(c. 1879)

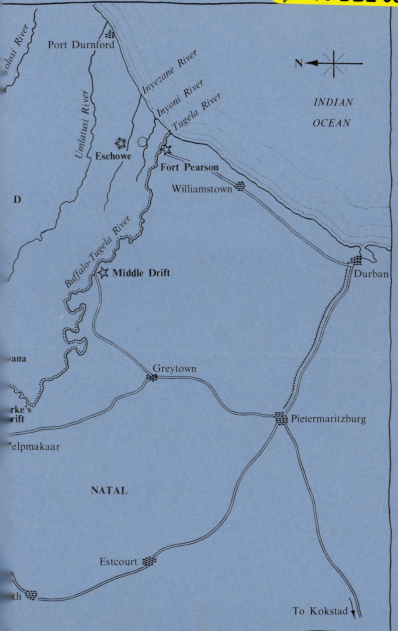

Zolosi River

Port Durnford

Umlatusi River

Inyezane River

Inyoni River

Tugela River

N

INDIAN OCEAN

Eschowe

Fort Pearson

Williamstown

D

Buffalo-Tugela River

Middle Drift

Durban

vana

Greytown

rke's
rift

elpmakaar

Pietermaritzburg

NATAL

Estcourt

th

To Kokstad

THE ZULU WAR

1879

THE ZULU WAR

1879

by

Alan Lloyd

Hart-Davis, MacGibbon London

Granada Publishing Limited
First published in Great Britain 1973 by Hart-Davis MacGibbon Ltd
Park Street St Albans Hertfordshire and
3 Upper James Street London W1R 4BP

Second impression 1974

ISBN 0 246 10560 7
Printed in Great Britain by
Fletcher & Son Ltd
Norwich

To
unforgotten stablemates
of 605 Squadron

CONTENTS

❦

LIST OF ILLUSTRATIONS

Maps

The illustrations used in this book were provided by
Illustration Research Service.

Chapter One

SIR BARTLE
KNOWS BEST

❦

> *Wider still and wider shall thy bounds be set;*
> *God who made thee mighty, make thee mightier yet.*
>
> Arthur Christopher Benson,
> 'Land of Hope ond Glory'

AT the opening of 1879, in circumstances of some enduring mystery, Frederick Augustus Thesiger, General Lord Chelmsford, eldest son of the former Lord Chancellor of England, led a British army from Natal into uncharted Zululand, a fringe of that empire on which the sun was yet to set.

Today, as a province of the Republic of South Africa, Natal and Zululand are conjoined, the wider bounds marked by the Indian Ocean to the east, Cape Province to the south, Basutoland, the Orange Free State and the Transvaal to the west, Swaziland and Mozambique to the north. At the time of Chelmsford's expedition, however, Natal stopped south of Zululand, in the region of the Tugela river.

In the European context, its history was limited. The early Portuguese adventurers had largely ignored the territory, though Vasco da Gama, sighting the coast en route to India, named it Terra Natalis. Its reputation as a storm area disenchanted many seamen. Indeed, the white man's introduction to Natal was not auspicious. The first party known to have penetrated the interior was of shipwrecked Portuguese who reached safety by a hazardous slog through Zululand and Tongaland to Lourenço Marques. Later, a temporary shanty fort was established on the coast by survivors of two other doomed ships, an English slaver and a Dutch trader.

In 1689, and again in 1721, the Dutch attempted to secure Natal Bay, but both moves were quickly abandoned. The coast was difficult, while there seemed no swift profits to be had from the country. Moreover, the sub-tropical shores were malarial, the rising hinterland subject to severe droughts. For a further century, Natal was neglected by the speculators of maritime Europe, then Britain's occupation of the southern Cape provided a base for closer exploration.

It proved Natal a more enticing land than had been supposed. Grazing was plentiful, game abounded, the flora was vividly beautiful. Climatically, the region varied appreciably. No one was going to make a fortune there overnight, but in the long term it was a property well worth developing. In 1835, the initial settlers founded a municipality at their landing point and main depot, naming it Durban after the then Governor at Cape Town, Sir Benjamin D'Urban.

Pioneering was hard; the men who undertook it, harder. A motley crowd of farmers, traders and soldiers of fortune, they contrived not only to cajole large numbers of the African occupants into fixed locations but to impose a hut tax on them which, for many years, was the most stable revenue of the colony. The preservation of peace with the tribesmen of Natal, who hugely outnumbered the encroaching foreigners, was a remarkable accomplishment, but the British hesitated to push their luck beyond the Tugela. The reputation of the Zulu people was formidable. Only with the arrival of Chelmsford and imperial soldiers were the tendrils of empire offered north.

To the rough and ready settlers, Lord Chelmsford was a rare bird. A hook-nosed gentleman of aristocratic bearing with a long, spindly frame between his whiskers and his riding boots, he had entered the service of Her Majesty thirty-five years earlier, as an officer of the Grenadier Guards. In his younger days, he had seen action in a number of the bloody and bumbling conflicts which had soiled the pink frontiers of the world map, but, for the last ten years or so, had been concerned with administration, as adjutant-general in India.

A pen and ink sketch of his lordship in Zululand, executed by a fellow officer, shows him gaunt and bearded, one thin leg braced, one hand in pocket, stretching forward a scrawny neck to inspect the terrain through field-glasses. Ahead lay ten thousand square miles of scrubby coastal plain, sloping parkland, broken hills and high prairies rising in terraces from the Indian Ocean west to the Drakensberg, and intersected by numerous fast-flowing rivers.

It was not *darkest* Africa, but in the popular mythology of nineteenth-century Europe the whole of the southern continent was populated by depraved barbarians whose intentions were as black as their naked bodies, and Chelmsford plied his glasses earnestly. There is something about the portrait irresistibly reminiscent of Don Quixote, a comparison not entirely confined to his appearance, for no one has ever doubted that his lordship's integrity was as unimpeachable as his fortunes were varied.

Chelmsford's army – 18,000 strong, or thereabouts, of which half was European – entered the little-known land of the Zulus in the finest style of Victoria's legions, resplendent in scarlet and blue, helmets gull white, bayonets and horses burnished, regimental bands playing march-time. Not that it was all tart and no teeth. Breech-loading rifles, now universally adopted by the imperial infantry, provided their ranks with an overwhelming superiority against the muzzle-loaders of less resourceful enemies. Hale's rocket, a tube-fired projectile carried by Chelmsford's men, was both physically devastating and psychologically demoralising, a weapon that had already wrought terror among unsophisticated tribesmen. Then there was a battery of seven-pounder field guns, and the crank-operated Gatling *mitrailleuse*, one of the most formidable innovations of the seventies, capable, it was reputed, of discharging upward of a hundred rounds a minute with immaculate accuracy. Its handlers called it affectionately 'the bulldog'.

In ammunition from shell to small-bore, the invaders were equipped to eliminate the 150,000 population of Zululand many times over. Since the Zulu warrior still relied basically on his spear and a hide shield, Chelmsford's incursion – aimed at the royal kraal of Ulundi, some seventy miles from the border – was regarded complacently, even enthusiastically, by its personnel.

Observed one stoic correspondent with the strike force: 'Field services, with, please Providence, some genuine fighting experience thrown in, evokes the finest qualities of the soldier. It forges the true link of mutual good feeling between officers and men; it stimulates *esprit de corps*; it brings good men to the front, and incites men less good to emulate the fine examples they see before them; it blots out the baser phases of garrison life at home; it teaches self-reliance, manliness, and a rude homely patriotism quite different from the gassy swagger of the music hall.'

Providential or otherwise, the lessons to be learned from the 'genuine fighting experience' portended were to prove more traumatic. All too soon, for too many, 'the baser phases of garrison life' would seem a sweet dream. 'Homely patriotism' was in for a nasty shock. Among the many questions raised by what can best be described as the extraordinary Grand Guignol to unfold in Zululand – and neither government nor administration would be unscathed – not the least perplexing arises at the outset; by what reason was Chelmsford there in the first place?

When Lord Chelmsford (then the Hon. F. A. Thesiger) had assumed command of the British forces in South Africa in March 1878, he could not have been long discerning a divergence of administrative opinion regarding the Zulus. Notable in their conflicting attitudes towards the neighbouring African nation were Sir Henry Bulwer, the Governor of Natal, a man of cautious and diplomatic tendencies, and the High Commissioner of South Africa, Sir Bartle Frere, a square-jawed, walrus-moustached apostle of imperial expansion.

In the Zulu king, Cetshwayo, these two found a focal point for their differences. While Bulwer praised the monarch's patience and forbearance, Frere abused him as a 'sanguinary tyrant' and 'bloodthirsty despot'. Since the few who knew the king well included neither of these gentlemen, and none has left a convincing reference, Cetshwayo remains largely conjectural in character. Physically, he was a powerful man, then of middle age, whose small head and fine Hamitic features perched pea-like above a paunchy torso and huge thighs. On the balance of evidence, he emerges a prudent politician whose worst failing, in retrospect, was procrastination. Like Philip II of Spain, he regarded time as his ally. Unfortunately for Cetshwayo, black time and white time were not synchronised.

Cetshwayo had succeeded his father to the Zulu throne five years earlier. At his coronation, to which a colonial representative, Theophilus Shepstone, was invited, the new king gave assurances of his goodwill towards the British in Natal, his southern neighbours. Shepstone, in return, pledged support from his masters.

The black monarch remained friendly to the British. Indeed, at least partly aware of their resources, mere pragmatism would have inclined him to do so. Others, however, strained his cordiality. Land-hungry and acquisitive, the Boers of the Transvaal had been encroaching on the northern border since the days of his father, who, they asserted, had ceded them a large tract of Zululand. This claim, strenuously denied by Cetshwayo and his parent before him, was backed by armed coercion and blackmail. The Boers flourished a printed contract, but since the Zulu rulers were illiterate its value was dubious. In 1875, having confined his reaction to repeated requests for British backing, the king's position became critical. The Transvaal Republic was moving to annex the disputed land.

Natal could no longer stay indifferent. While the Boers were warned of the dangers in their aggressive policy, Bulwer exerted his diplomacy to soothe Cetshwayo, profusely complimenting the king on his restraint and moderation. Two years later, the Zulu monarch still holding his hand, the Boers still pushing, Britain annexed the Transvaal rather than – as Shepstone put it – see the republic provoke the native races to a war which might imperil the entire white population of South Africa. Cetshwayo's boundary complaints against the Boers now became a matter of direct negotiation with the British Government, which, a week or so before Chelmsford arrived in the colony, appointed a committee of inquiry to resolve the matter.

It might thus have been supposed, since the demonstrably patient Cetshwayo welcomed the inquiry gratefully, that events were moving towards settlement. Such a surmise reckoned without Sir Bartle Frere. A man of fixed ideas on foreign relations, Frere believed strongly that the native states on the doorstep of the empire – especially those prone, as he saw the Zulus, to 'unmitigated barbarism' – should retain their independence, if at all, under British sufferance. This precluded, in Frere's mind, the maintenance of armies by these neighbouring nations. Opined the High Commissioner: 'While he (Cetshwayo) keeps up a large standing army, useless for all but purposes of tyranny and aggression, it is impossible for his peaceful neighbours to feel secure.'

From the moment Chelmsford took command of the British forces in South Africa, Frere was urging preparations for a confrontation with the Zulu king, besieging Her Majesty's Government with demands for more troops. These the colonial office, not unaware of the High Commissioner's peculiar propensities, refused as unnecessary. Britain was already painfully embroiled in a brutal and protracted conflict on the north-west frontier of India, no little aggravated some years earlier by a member of the India Council who had recommended the establishment of British officers and forces in Afghanistan. By a notable coincidence, that member had been Sir Bartle Frere.

Nor had Britain's armed adventures in Africa of recent years proved less embarrassing. In 1867, Lord Napier had embarked on an expedition to Magdala in Abyssinia which had proved successful but highly explosive. Chelmsford had gone with him. In 1874, a punitive expedition to Ashanti, inland of the Gold Coast, had extricated itself by the skin of its teeth and the skill of Britain's outstanding general, Sir Garnet Wolseley. The Ashanti capital, Kumasi, had been burnt and a war indemnity demanded from its government. Within a couple of years, the Ashantis had rebuilt most of Kumasi, conveniently forgotten about paying the indemnity and were again causing sleepless nights on the Gold Coast. Though both ventures had been claimed as triumphs of British arms, they were such triumphs as Westminster had no compelling urge to see repeated.

In the July following Chelmsford's arrival in South Africa, the boundary inquiry commission forwarded its report to Sir Bartle Frere. To the High Commissioner's horror, its findings were entirely in Cetshwayo's favour. Its decision, in short, was that the disputed land belonged to the Zulus, that no cession of territory had ever been made by them, and that, even had such a cession been made, it would have been null and void unless confirmed by the voice of the nation.

Indignantly, Frere now looked to Bulwer to join him in refuting the commission's findings. In a long correspondence between the two men, Frere strove to invalidate the report with a number of specious arguments, typical of which was the assertion that the Zulus formed a migratory tribe with no settled boundaries. In fact, they had been settled in Zululand since at least the end of the seventeenth century – probably as far back as the early colonisation of North America – and certainly anteceded European settlement in Natal and the Transvaal. Bulwer, refusing to be browbeaten on the issue, insisted that British faith had been committed. In the face of such obduracy, the High Commissioner could not wholly reject the report. Instead, while eventually allowing Zulu ownership of the disputed lands, he conceived the proviso that the rights of individuals and private property on those lands should be placed under the charge of a British resident who would keep a general eye on Cetshwayo's administration.

In other words, the Boer settlers were to be left in possession under British protection, with the added insult that the representative of a foreign government was to snoop on the internal affairs of an independent nation. Not surprisingly, there seems to have been no rush to impart this proposition to the Zulus. While the loaded findings awaited transmission, Frere continued his military preparations, at the same time snatching avidly at anything which supported his vilification of Cetshwayo, the king of 'faithless and cruel character', as he called him in August. Nothing in the monarch's record impressed the High Commissioner. 'As far as I have heard,' he exclaimed inscrutably, 'his highest aspiration is in shedding blood.'

Three episodes roused Frere to proclamations of high affront, serving later to bolster the war faction and its apologists. Widely and imaginatively reported for European consumption, the so-called Sirayo affair, the Middle Drift incident and the missionary dispute are worth considering only as examples of confusion between cultural attitudes. The first resulted from the adultery of two wives of a Zulu chief named Sirayo. Having been discovered in their intrigues, these women fled to Natal pursued by Sirayo's sons who, with some sense of legal nicety, dragged them back across the border before satisfying honour. This involved a brutal double murder. A flagrant instance, it seemed to the glass house of Victorian opinion, of the African's abuse of the female sex.

Actually, the Zulus – indeed, the whole Nguni group of the Bantu people, to which they belonged – greatly esteemed their womenfolk. Elaborate maidens' guilds, headed by elected 'queens', existed to preserve the honour of unmarried girls, and to ensure sharp retribution to anyone who threatened or slandered it. Once wed, the Zulu girl was seldom neglected by her husband. It was a point of pride with the men to keep their wives sexually satisfied. To do so, while restricting pregnancies to intervals of several years, they cultivated refined skills as lovers. Nineteenth-century Zulu women, strong and buxom, working the gardens and relishing the attentions of their spouses, had some cause to feel complacent. But the infringement of Zulu codes was often harshly punished, and adultery, regarded as an indefensible personal and social affront, was penalised by death.

Shocked by the killings of the two wives, the Governor of Natal requested that Cetshwayo should deliver the youths for trial and punishment. To Cetshwayo it seemed that no more than justice had been done; nevertheless, on the advice of an English trader named John Dunn, who had insinuated himself at the Zulu court, the king offered £50 as compensation for any offence to the colonists. This Bulwer refused – though not disinclined to settle for a larger sum.

None of which much excited the British Government. As Sir Michael Hicks Beach, Secretary of State for the Colonies, observed without excessive interest, 'there was nothing in Cetshwayo's conduct which would preclude the hope of a satisfactory arrangement'. Sir Bartle Frere thought otherwise. Unless the murderers were yielded with apologies, Frere thundered, there could be little hope of pacific relations with the Zulus. An even wider gulf between the High Commissioner and the home authorities was evinced in the Middle Drift incident. The drift, or ford, concerned was on the lower Tugela, the river (known at a higher point as the Buffalo) which marked the border between Natal and Zululand. A surveyor of the colonial engineer's department was inspecting a road in the area when he and his assistants were approached by Zulus who wished to know – perhaps reasonably, since a sudden interest in the little-used border trail could hardly fail to appertain to their own land – what was going on. When the surveyor told them to get lost, the Zulus seized his party and detained it a while, though without harm.

In the opinion of the Colonial Office, the behaviour of the natives was in no way sanctioned by the Zulu authorities, and was at least partly due to the indiscretion of the engineers. Frere took an entirely opposed view. It was, he proclaimed, a most serious injury and outrage, and should be dealt with severely.

The so-called missionary dispute was confused by the vagueness and generalisation of the accusations, and by contradictions on all sides. The missionaries involved were Norwegians. They had been some time in Zululand, apparently suffering little or no molestation, when they suddenly decided to retire from the country. The reason they gave was that their converts had been maltreated by Cetshwayo. Here was a theme the High Commissioner could work on, if not readily substantiate. 'One gentleman,' he declared hotly, 'who had better means of obtaining the truth than anyone else, told me he had no doubt the number of converts killed was considerable, though many were killed ostensibly for other causes . . . He gave me this and much more information under a stipulation that his name should not be mentioned.'

On the other hand, the official representative of the missions in Zululand, who had no qualms about his name, Oftebro, being mentioned, asserted that the missionaries left the country on the advice of the British official Theophilus Shepstone, in expectation of a political crisis between the Zulus and the colonists. Bulwer believed that, while Cetshwayo had never been in favour of missionaries, 'there has not been any actual expulsion of missionaries by the Zulu king ... he has not gone back from what he said'.

The king himself was ambivalent. While professing to welcome the opportunity of wider education presented by the missions, he found it hard to accept what he saw as the insolence and affected superiority of the converts. Cetshwayo would have been glad to encourage the missionaries, he implied, had they confined their teaching to subjects consonant with Zulu social mores. Of course, this was not possible. The missionary ethic impinged on every aspect of local life – domestic, political and legal, as well as religious. All the bad characters in the land, complained the monarch, could flout his authority on the pretext of being Christians. Missionary proselytisation was subversive to Zulu justice.

Again, Frere denounced the ignorance, cruelty and treachery of Cetshwayo, and called for his punishment. Again, Bulwer opposed him on many points. Not only Bulwer, but the British Government, was concerned that the High Commissioner's aggressive attitude, especially the military preparations he was urging on Chelmsford, should not exacerbate an already alarmed Zulu nation. The Colonial Office was quite clearly for lowering, not increasing, the tension.

'Her Majesty's Government,' wrote Hicks Beach, rejecting Frere's application for extra regiments, 'are not prepared to comply with the request for a reinforcement of troops. All the information that has hitherto reached them with respect to Zululand appears to them to justify a confident hope that by the exercise of prudence, and by meeting the Zulus in a spirit of forbearance and reasonable compromise, it will be possible to avert the very serious evil of a war with Cetshwayo.'

Incensed by the refusal, Frere wrote letter after letter urging the Government to change its mind. Chelmsford supported the demand for extra troops. At last, the Government yielded in detail. Towards the end of November, it was announced that reinforcements would be provided, but on the firm understanding that they should not be used aggressively. Still, the bulk of white settlers on the border seems not to have shared Frere's view of the Zulu threat. According to a veteran Natal resident who visited the boundary territories in October, at the height of a severe drought:

> Wherever I went, the want of water was the chief topic of conversation. The Zulus were very little talked about ... Arrived at Utrecht (a frontier town in the north) I found that fear of the Zulus was the last thing that entered the heads of the townspeople. They seem to feel quite secure, and, ignorant of the intentions of the government, will not believe themselves in danger of attack ... I am convinced that the nearer one gets to Maritzburg (i.e. the further from Zululand) the more alarming will be found the reports. Near the border, even reasonable security is felt. But I mention that some Boers are very fond of spreading reports of aggression, which I believe exist only in their own fears and passions.

If fears and passions were natural to uninvited settlement in foreign lands, they were not the only motives backing the white hawks. Zulu military conscription, traditionally embracing the great majority of able-bodied men in the nation, posed an obstacle to colonial development more profound than its primitive weaponry. In order to grow and prosper, the European communities in south-east Africa needed native labour. Shepstone, after attending Cetshwayo's coronation, had reported regretfully that the Zulu were so 'attached' to their regimental system* that the recruitment of labour from that people was impossible. Until the system was destroyed, there could be no surplus of manpower there for colonial utilisation.

Among lesser factors militating in favour of a British offensive was the business to be done with the military commissariat, not least by haulage contractors whose wagons would be needed by the hundred. The supply demands of a campaign could bring a boon to the provision and transport industries, and many in Natal whiffed a profitable enterprise. Meanwhile, as Frere and Chelmsford advanced their martial preparations, the award of the

---

* See p. 29 *et seq.* and pp. 51-2.

boundary commission languished in the High Commissioner's office. It was only when Frere received a sharp rebuke from the Colonial Secretary that he condescended to send his envoys to the Tugela to relay the findings of the inquiry to the king's representatives – getting on for five months after he had received the report. The meeting took place on 11 December. Chelmsford's forces were ready, and the ultimatum composed which would lead to the Zulu War.

The Zulu indunas, or state officials, assembled at the Tugela to meet Frere's men had scarcely absorbed the favourable land awards, when the High Commissioner's ultimatum was passed to them. It quickly cancelled their gratification. Frere demanded, within a space of twenty days, the surrender of the Sirayo sons, five hundred head of cattle for the delay in delivering them, and a further hundred head of cattle as atonement for the Middle Drift incident.

If that surprised the State officials, the rest was beyond belief. In brief, Frere decreed: (1) that Cetshwayo should disband the Zulu army and put an end to the nation's military system; (2) that the king should allow the missionaries to return to Zululand without restraint or condition; (3) that he should receive a British resident. If these demands were not met within thirty days, Cetshwayo was to understand that the British army would invade to enforce them.

That the king could accept such an ultimatum and retain his credibility as the head of a sovereign nation was, as Frere cannot have failed to appreciate, unthinkable. It was an invitation to war by premeditated insult, and as such the indunas refused to deliver it. The document was therefore thrust on a native attendant. Prudently, the man got rid of it to the safest intermediary he could think of: the English adventurer Dunn, who enjoyed a gift of land from Cetshwayo within the Zulu boundary. Dunn, perceiving it too hot to handle, read it hastily to some messengers, despatched them to the royal kraal at Ulundi, and promptly abandoned the manuscript. On his later evidence, the king never received the official ultimatum, and was unlikely to have heard more than a garbled version from the messengers.

Not that it mattered much, anyway. Frere was not overconcerned with the finer points. On 6 January 1879, notwithstanding a request for more time from Cetshwayo, and in the absence of a formal rejection of Frere's terms, the first British forces moved into Zululand – four days before the stipulated period of grace expired.

Chapter Two

BLACK KINGS, WHITE TRAVELLERS

Ah! King George's warriors are a fine set of men. In fact, King George and I are brothers: he has conquered all the whites, and I have subdued all the blacks. Is King George as handsome as I am?

Shaka on learning of George IV from H. F. Fynn, the first Englishman at the Zulu court.

THERE is a succinct Zulu idiom – *Wo! ngi hudelwa yi hubulu!* (Alas! I have been excreted on by a raven!) – to describe unexpected misfortune. Frere's ultimatum descended on Cetshwayo from a blue sky at the time of the Festival of First Fruits, the little *umkosi*, a period traditionally set in Zululand for the promulgation of new laws and the reviewing of the army, together with dancing, singing and much general happiness. The shadow of the raven now darkened the festivities. Throughout the kingdom, people awaited the word of the king's council.

The administrative machinery of the Zulu state operated through delegated authority, with diminishing executive power, in a pyramidal structure: nation to tribe, tribe to tribal district, and thence to the homesteads, the scattered kraals from which the cattle were herded and the gardens worked. The system was 'casteless'. All men – allowing for the authority of their leaders – were deemed equal and entitled to a share of the tribal lands. In turn, each owed allegiance to the sovereign, the symbol of

24

nationhood, who headed the government. It was a trusted scheme. The imminence of invasion occasioned no panic. Half a century earlier, one of the first Europeans to visit the country, a trader named Henry Fynn, had remarked on the 'astonishing orderliness' of the populace.

A. T. Bryant, pre-eminent historian of the nation, who lived in Zululand shortly after the Zulu War, corroborated this evidence, listing submission to authority, obedience to the law, respect for superiors, order and self-restraint, fearlessness and self-sacrifice, constant work and civic duty as 'the very foundation stones' of Zulu society. Add to these intriguingly Victorian attributes a strong military tradition, accompanied by a system of discipline by no means less stringent than the shootings, hangings and floggings imposed by the British administration, and it is not difficult to agree with Bryant that the social arrangements of the Zulu were 'surprisingly like our own'.

Phlegmatic and dignified, with a dry sense of humour, Bartle Frere's 'ignorant savages' took an ironic delight in recalling how one Zulu monarch, on learning that it rained a lot in England, had advised that the British king should stop trying to keep his powder dry and arm his guards instead with Zulu spears.

The Zulu belonged to a broad family of people called the Bantu, groups of which had begun moving into South Africa from the north perhaps in the twelfth or thirteenth centuries AD. Until then, the land had been occupied by the closely related Bushmen and Hottentots, small in stature with yellowish-brown skins, who lived by hunting, foraging and, in the case of the Hottentots, on sheep and cattle, too. Neither of these peoples practised agriculture, which, as a feature of the more varied economy of the Bantu, enabled the latter to live in larger and more sophisticated societies.

Taller and darker than the stocky hunters who preceded them, the encroaching Bantu gradually dominated the southern lands, sometimes expelling the existing communities, sometimes absorbing them, occasionally living with them as neighbours. Though less primitive than the Bushmen, the newcomers hardly led an easy life. Despite the many rivers they encountered, they had not learned to build boats, nor did they know the wheel. Their huts were mostly bare, they had little warm covering against the cold southern nights, the cause and treatment of sickness was poorly understood. Much illness was put down to witchcraft, with the consequence that witch-hunting, especially during the sickness of an important person, led to the execution of many innocents, often with atrocious cruelty.

The Bantu people who penetrated Zululand and Natal belonged to a language group known as the Nguni, its tribes varying in dialect but understanding each other's tongue, also sharing much general culture. Members of the Nguni group had reached south of Natal by 1300 — possibly a good deal earlier, according to Professor Omer-Cooper, an expert on the history of Bantu Africa whose observations are followed here.

The Nguni primarily were cattle men, but they grew crops of millet, and later maize, which were tended by the women and stored, in times of surplus, in covered pits. The cattle, providing meat, milk and hide, were the chief currency of the tribes, and objects of sacrifice at religious observances. The cattle enclosure, or kraal, was at the heart of the Nguni community. This might comprise an isolated hamlet, largely of one family, or a sizeable settlement of many family compounds.

The Nguni family was often complex, for marriage was commonly polygamous and the wives of a single husband were separated into households of varying prestige and privilege. Beyond the basic family, those sharing ancestry on the male side formed a clan, with a chief who ranked above the heads of family.

From the clan, enlarged by adherents outside the central stock, evolved the tribe, with perhaps a few thousand members. At core, this was a kinship group, but overall it was a form of elementary state, the central lineage enjoying aristocratic status and providing the chief, his council and other tribal officers. The position of the Nguni chief was an exalted one. Simultaneously the head of civil, religious, judicial and military affairs of the tribe, he was the supreme arbiter of the legal and political matters of the community. At the same time, since his ancestors were esteemed the guardian spirits of the people, his role was central to all sacred and magical rituals.

But his rule was not absolute. However powerful, the chief was expected to govern in consultation with his advisers and with regard to custom and public opinion. Vital decisions, for instance that of making war, were discussed at a great council of community leaders. An unpopular chief might well find his people slipping away to join a happier tribe, while a really oppressive chief would probably end up assassinated and replaced by an ambitious relative. Such sanctions, while rough and ready, were not ineffective.

It was the chief's responsibility to apportion the tribal territory among his followers, individuals holding land more or less permanently, subject to their lawful behaviour. Provincial communities within the area were normally administered for the chief by his close family, the chief himself maintaining households in different quarters of the tribal lands. Such a family hierarchy made for internal feuds. Succession to the chieftainship was commonly disputed, and tribes frequently divided under rival leaders into independent states.

Later, the process would be reversed to become, dramatically in the case of the Zulu tribe, one of unification, but in the early days of the southern Bantu it was not inconsistent with successful colonisation in a region of abundant land and small-scale opposition. At this stage, warfare between rival Bantu tribes, if not infrequent, was of limited severity and involved little loss of life. According to Omer-Cooper: 'The purification rites which a warrior had to undergo after killing an enemy, even in open war, suggest a fundamental respect for human life and an ethos which regarded peace as the norm.'

Observations by a party of shipwreck survivors who spent a year with the southern Nguni during the seventeenth century led the Dutch commander Simon van der Stell to conclude: 'It would be impossible to buy any slaves there, for they would not part with their children, or any of their connections, for anything in the world ... Revenge has little place in their lives since it is obligatory to submit disputes to the king, who, having heard the parties, gives sentence on the spot, to which all submit without murmur ... The kings are much respected and beloved ... Of their courage, little can be adduced, for during the stay of the Netherlanders among them they had no wars.'

At the beginning of the nineteenth century, the Zulu had been a relatively unimportant tribe of the Nguni, perhaps two thousand people, living at the heart of what later became Zululand, on the White Umfolosi river. The dominant tribe in the region then was the Mtetwa, in the east above the Tugela, ruled by the paramount chief Dingiswayo, a resourceful and constructive man who was to have a profound influence on Zulu history. It was probably Dingiswayo who converted the old tribal circumcision guilds, the *ama Buto*, into the regimental system, at the same time adapting the horned-crescent hunting formation of the Nguni for military purposes. At all events, his power spread quickly over wide lands, at last embracing thirty chiefs, an embryo state he sought to embellish by opening trade with the merchant adventurers of Europe.

Among Dingiswayo's protégés was a young Zulu named Shaka who had fled his native tribe, accompanied by his mother, to escape the disfavour of his father, the chief Senzangakona. Shaka, enrolled in a Mtetwa regiment, soon impressed Dingiswayo with his outstanding physique, intelligence and bravery. Ambitious, bent on avenging the humiliation of his exile, Shaka reciprocated the paramount chief's admiration, emulating the aims and methods of his mentor. On the death of Senzangakona, it was reputedly Dingiswayo who engineered Shaka's succession to the Zulu throne.

In 1818, Dingiswayo was tricked and murdered by his enemy Zwide, chief of the powerful Ndwande. Shaka, leading his small force of Zulu to the rescue, was warned of ambush and escaped to await a day when he might settle with the triumphant Zwide. Meanwhile, he had to extend and consolidate his own rule. Assuming control of the leaderless and splitting Mtetwa people, Shaka improved the military system of Dingiswayo, introducing the stabbing assegai, placing emphasis on fitness and mobility, employing such adjuncts to his army as spies, scouts and decoys. Most significantly, in his role of general, Shaka swept south-east Africa of the concept of ritualised conflict, replacing it with the *impi ebomvu*, the red war, or war to the death.

Like most primitive people, the early Nguni had pursued their inter-tribal animosities largely by raiding. When honour demanded a showdown, the rival armies would array themselves a short distance from each other where, in the manner of feuding school-boys, they tended to 'act out' their hostility in a bravura display of relatively harmless gesture and insult. This effectively conservationist procedure might be accompanied by a desultory throwing of spears, and isolated clashes between individuals, but seldom produced defeat or victory in real terms.

As competition for land and power intensified, ritualised war-fare became inadequate. The need was no longer for aggression therapy but for decisive action, and Shaka was quick to adjust to the pressures. Instead of throwing their spears at an enemy who usually dodged them, Shaka's warriors were taught to charge forward and stab, a technique as dismaying to their opponents as it was revolutionary. With a fit, disciplined army, accomplished in flanking tactics and trained to close, to pursue, to kill relentlessly, Shaka embarked on a career of conquest which, subjecting or vanquishing all foes, raised the Zulu from a minor tribe to a nation. The war cry of his warriors, *Si-gi-di!* (One thousand! i.e., He who is equal to a thousand) became feared from the Cape to Swaziland.

In 1819, Shaka avenged the murder of Dingiswayo by over-whelming Zwide and the Ndwande. By 1824, when the first Englishman paid an apprehensive visit to his empire, he is reputed to have commanded fifteen regiments and ruled fifty thousand people, thousands more having fled Natal to Matabeleland and Pondoland to escape his depredations.

A legend in his own time, the first Zulu monarch rapidly assumed bizarre proportions in South African folklore, an imaginative mythology generously coloured with blood and diabolism. Victorian writers (and some later ones), intent on justifying European intervention in Zululand, elaborated the Shaka legend to support the theory of military fanaticism in that country. Among other apocryphal anecdotes given wide credence was the tale that Shaka ordered the execution of an entire Zulu regiment, allegedly the 'Umkandhlu', for retreating. Though in this case not only the event but the regiment lacked substance, his use of the death sentence was certainly arbitrary and frequent to the point of promiscuity.

Like many dynamic rulers, Shaka appears to have been a heady blend of contradictions, at once scrupulous and ruthless, impulsive and prudent, cruel and compassionate. He treated the first Englishmen at his court, a small and vulnerable group of adventurers headed by Henry Fynn, with courtesy, yet they were appalled by his seemingly mercurial behaviour towards his subjects. One moment he was risking his life in a torrent to save their children and cattle from drowning; the next, he was casually ordering their death for minor misdemeanours.

To his enemies, his message was unequivocal: submit or be eliminated. On the other hand, he emerges from the evidence as neither sadist nor psychopath. He did not care, for the most part, to witness the executions he ordered, and sometimes showed real remorse. His constant impulsion – the desire to deter rivals and instil obedience and uniformity in a mixed and factious populace – was not a depravity, nor his penal code outrageous in the context of a people who believed implicitly that death was the beginning of a better life, and who would unquestionably have regarded it as preferable to the incarceration enforced in Britain for minor crimes.

Shaka regarded Fynn and company with a mixture of admiration, kindliness and amused tolerance, attitudes his guests promptly repaid by attempting to defraud his people of large tracts of their native land under guise of a document the king could neither read nor was induced to understand. For all that, he encouraged and patronised British settlement of Port Natal and its hinterland. Four years after befriending the white men, he was assassinated at an audience by two of his half-brothers, Dingane and Mhlangana. According to Zulu oral tradition, there was little glee when the news spread. People rushed from their huts wailing: *Ku dilike intaba! Inkosi ye lizwe ishonile!* (The mountain has collapsed! The lord of the world is dead!) Catastrophe, many were convinced, would follow Shaka's death.

To the extent that his successor, Dingane, initiated the first armed clash between the Zulu people and encroaching white interests, his reign could at least be said to have augured that catastrophe. Europe heaped him with opprobrium. 'Dingane,' pronounced Bishop Schreuder, the Norwegian missionary who 'enlightened' Frere on Zulu history, 'was simply a beast on two legs'. Admittedly, as a national symbol, a figure of epic venturing, he fell far short of Shaka. He had neither the athletic proclivities nor the intellect of his brother, preferring indolence to activity, the congenial company of court sycophants to a barrack life. From a Zulu point of view, he was retrograde.

Yet it might well have been expected that the voice of white expansion would have welcomed him. His disposition was pacific and unambitious. He attempted no conquests, the only military adventures of his twelve-year-reign being relatively minor ones against African enemies. Possessing no martial capabilities, Dingane did not take part in them. Wrote an acquaintance: 'There is nothing sanguinary in his appearance.' A luxuriant obesity gave the real clue to him.

Captain Allen Gardiner, naval officer cum self-appointed apostle, and founder of the earliest Christian mission in Natal, very quickly took the measure of Dingane. At their first meeting, the king showed no interest in the gospels. Returning with a liberal inducement of silken sword-belts, gilt bracelets and coloured ribbons, Gardiner was immediately granted permission to preach in Zululand, and was actually proclaimed a landed chief. A year later, three American missionaries, Adam, Grout and Champion, were also allowed to open stations in the country. At one stage, Dingane himself took lessons in Bible reading. Unsurprisingly, since the Zulu knew nothing of writing, let alone English, he rather quickly gave up.

Neither his eschewal of the conquering mantle of his brother, nor his patronage of the mission stations, was to temper the European view of Dingane. Even Bryant, who regarded Shaka as a great man, dismissed his successor as a black 'fiend'. In part, this was because for the first time at Dingane's accession many white settlers saw the particularly vicious in-fighting of African politics at close hand. Having secured the throne by murder, Dingane proceeded to the traditional task of ridding himself not only of his enemies, but also of such friends and relatives as might be strong enough one day to rival him. Remarkably, he spared two of the most obvious candidates, his younger brothers Mpande, or Panda, and Gqugqu.

If the new king's cynical resort to pre-emptive assassination struck his European neighbours as perfidious (to the Zulu, it was political reality), the real shock was yet to come. Dingane's coronation pronouncement to his people had promised them happiness, prosperity and peace, in the pursuit of which he proposed an increasing trade in hide, horns and ivory with the British at Port Natal. From the start, a certain rapport had been struck with these strange whites from Joji's (George's) land, whose milder eccentricities appealed to the Zulu. Fynn had arrived at Shaka's court in tatters, barefoot, his head surmounted by a crownless straw hat. There had been an easy-going informality about their laissez-faire activities which reassured the natives.

In 1837, however, Dingane was visited by the vanguard of a different breed of white man, the Boer immigrants now crossing the Drakensberg from the Cape into Zululand. Dour, determined and well-armed, the Boers came not in the guise of accommodating traders from Europe, but as rugged cattlemen, hardened to the ways of Africa, resolved to move in, to expand and assert themselves. As Professor Hatterseley, the historian of Natal, observes, the Boer trekkers were 'a religious-minded people, well versed in the teaching of the Old Testament, which seemed to them to uphold racial inequality and justify summary discipline for the backward and heathen ... they concluded that the prestige and authority of the colonist must be upheld and the black man subjected to firm restraint'.

Though the search for fresh grazing had nudged the Boers from their Cape farms, the overwhelming motive of the Great Trek was the determination of the British Government to enforce equality before the law in its African territories. Still smarting at the loss of their slaves under the Act of 1833, the trekkers

streaming over the mountains brought no 'false ideals' of philan-
thropy to Zululand. From the first, the doctrine of black inferiority,
the principle of the colour bar, heavily underscored their intentions.

The Boer leader Piet Retief made contact with Dingane in
November, pressing for permission to settle on his southern lands.
This request was opposed by the king's missionary, Francis Owen
– who reminded Dingane that he had already made Gardiner chief
of the same lands – and more violently by Zulu advisers at the
royal court, who appear not to have been deluded by Boer
politeness. With a sly eye to his immediate benefit, Dingane left
decision conditional on the white men recovering for him some
cattle stolen by a Basuto robber chief.

It was no great problem for the mounted Boers. Indeed, the
efficiency with which they despatched the assignment can only
have emphasised the potential threat these hardy frontiersmen,
with their horses and firearms, posed for the apprehensive Zulus.
By the time Retief had returned with the cattle, Dingane had
resolved to destroy the newcomers before the influx assumed
irrepressible proportions. The grizzly method he chose accorded
with his own unheroic nature, and the notion, probably urged
on him by his magicians, that the Boers were evil sorcerers intent
on killing him. On 6 February 1838, despite warnings of treachery,
Retief, with sixty white followers and thirty Hottentot servants,
were invited into the kraal of Dingane's southern capital,
Mgungundlovu.

Sir William Harris, in his *Expedition into Southern Africa*,
described the rest as follows:

Three thousand Zulu warriors, standing up to dance, formed
a ring round them and for a time alternately retreated and
advanced in the customary manner until, upon a signal made
by Dingane (significantly, the order was 'Kill the wizards!'),
while the farmers were in the act of quaffing malt liquors,
which had been liberally handed round, rushed with one
accord upon their victims. The Dutchmen were dragged about
half a mile across the river by the hair of the head and,
their leader having been ostentatiously butchered, the Zulus
fell upon and despatched the rest.

The massacre at Mgungundlovu, and its immediate sequel, sparked a vendetta of mutual perfidy and distrust between the Zulu and their white neighbours which was to smoulder until the Zulu War fanned it to holocaust. While the missionary Owen, who had been in the region of the royal kraal 'reading his testament' as the slaughter of Retief was enacted, hastily prepared to flee Zululand with his American colleagues, Dingane's spearmen were moving with discomfiting speed to mop up the outlying Boer laagers. In a simultaneous attack on the wagon camps a few days after Retief's death, three hundred trekkers, men, women and children, perished.

A second Boer leader, Piets Uys, descending from the mountains at the head of a mounted force, was trapped and killed, his men routed. Meanwhile, a thrustful faction of the unofficial British settlement at Port Natal, disavowing the humanitarian sentiment prevailing in official quarters, had welcomed the Boers as men of like mind in their attitude to the blacks. With a body of Bantu levies, these Britons marched to the assistance of the trekkers, only to be decimated by Zulu spears on the Tugela. The remainder of the British colony was now obliged to take refuge aboard ship.

Receiving news of these tragic occurrences, the British Government could no longer ignore the situation in Natal. Though continuing to regard the Port settlement as 'an assemblage of British subjects living in a foreign country', it authorised the Cape establishment to despatch a small contingent of troops to the area. Their purpose was two-fold. In the first place, it was hoped they would stop the bloodshed. In the second place, by preventing the importation of gunpowder and essential stores to Natal, they might reduce its attraction to the trekkers, thus staunching the exodus from the Cape and preventing the invasion of native rights. In the event, neither purpose was realised. The troops arrived too late to prevent further fighting, while the Boers soon found other supply routes.

In the December following the Mgungundlovu massacre, Boer reinforcements, strengthened by a regrouped detachment of British settlers, advanced on Dingane to press the issue. With six hundred horse and two cannon, the Boer commander, Andries Pretorius, took station on the Ncome, afterwards called Blood River. Two flanks were protected by water, and wagons linked in a tight shielding laager. At dawn on the 16th (later known as Dingane's Day), the Zulu regiments attacked in close formation. Pretorius, an experienced fighter, controlled his men calmly, holding fire until the range was point-blank, then unleashing a devastating volley from the smooth-bore flintlocks.

Charging with courageous but imprudent resolution over ground carefully picked by their opponents, the Zulus fell in hundreds. After two hours, shaken and confused by their first sustained battle against musket and cannon fire, the black regiments broke and the Boer horsemen scattered them. Against severe Zulu losses, trekker casualties were negligible. When Dingane absorbed the implications of the outcome, he burned the fateful kraal at Mgungundlovu and moved his court north, establishing a new base near the Ngome forest.

If the formidable increase in white strength in Natal had sickened him of the south, the rest of the kingdom remained inviolate, and his army was still considerable. In a flash of unusual ambition, he even projected an expansion of his realm into Swaziland. It never materialised. He was still planning when the unbelievable happened – a mighty host of rebel Zulu appeared on the skyline, its bristling ranks backed by Boer horsemen with their long guns.

Shocked by the novel and disturbing events of Dingane's reign, a substantial body of Zulus (about 17,000) had followed his brother Mpande across the Tugela into Natal, where, to the distinct relief of the Boer settlers, the rebels struck a bargain with them. Mpande and his men would recross the river if the settlers would help them to overthrow Dingane. The result was the battle of Magongo, January 1840, in which the combined forces of Mpande and Pretorius defeated the king's regiments. While the brunt of the fighting was borne by Mpande's impi, or army, the psychological impact of a white commando in the rebel force probably swayed the issue. By an ironic turn of fate, Dingane fled to Swaziland, where he was murdered by the people he had planned to sub-jugate.

With Mpande crowned, the Boers exacted their price for sup-porting him. The former Zulu lands south of the Tugela were claimed republican territory, and the British detachment sent to discourage the trekkers was obliged to watch in some embarrass-ment as Natal fell increasingly under Boer influence. Three years later, the virtual revival of slavery in Boer methods of impress-ing native labour, together with the mounting commercial and strategic interest of south-east Africa, persuaded the British Government to annex Natal. Mpande was no trouble. On mis-sionary evidence a 'kindly and grateful' man, he ruled for thirty-two years at peace with the Natal administration, eventually – despite periodic internecine struggles – dying a natural death.

Cetshwayo, his succeeding son, though not sharing his father's indebtedness to white arms, continued to pursue pacific relations with his European neighbours. In the face of repeated Boer provo-cation, Cetshwayo maintained an attitude of restraint which, as has been noted, earned him not only the plaudits of the Governor of Natal, but a just reward from the belated boundary commission. At the same time, insistent on preserving the regimental strength without which his diplomacy must have been mere supplication, Cetshwayo earned the ire of those who would indeed have seen African kings as beggars at the white door.

'Since his installation,' wrote Frere in January 1879, the month of Chelmsford's invasion, 'Cetshwayo has endeavoured to build up a great military power, and to restore the system of Shaka by regulations seriously threatening his neighbours.' Yet 'the system' had never lapsed. Of the twenty-one regiments Chelmsford ascribed to the Zulus, one remained from Dingane's time and eighteen from Mpande's reign. Only two had been raised by Cetshwayo. Nor, on the available evidence, had the numerical strength of the army grown. Bishop Schreuder gave Mpande's army as 'about 40,000 soldiers'. Chelmsford reckoned Cetshwayo's army at about the same number. While both estimates, allowing for youthful initiates and retiring veterans, undoubtedly exceeded the effective fighting strength, the proportion of battle-worthy warriors is unlikely to have changed much.

The demand, after thirty-seven years of peace with the British, that this army should be disbanded, astounded Cetshwayo. It was a proposition, quite regardless of his own inclinations, he would never have dared put to the *i-bandla*, the state council. His first reactions to Frere's ultimatum were confused but non-violent – he temporised. Agreeing to surrender the principals of the Sirayo incident, and pay the fine asked in cattle, he requested an extension of the expiry date set by the Commissioner, explaining that the animals were scattered and his lands wide. Sir Bartle rejected the king's request.

When it dawned that the British were determined on a showdown, the royal council was outraged. Still, though many chiefs called for all-out hostilities against the colonies, Cetshwayo refrained from aggression, resolving to conduct a defensive war. According to Zulu accounts, he placed his hopes in a limited trial of strength, announcing his intention to 'fight on one day only' – a notion based on the traditional concept of a conclusive pitched battle. Understandably naïve in comprehension of British resources, the plan was confounded at the outset by an invasion on three fronts. It was not a single assegai, but a trident, that thrust into Zululand.

Chapter Three

THE WARRIORS

❦

The 'eathen in 'is blindness must end where 'e began,
But the backbone of the Army is the Non-commissioned
man!

Rudyard Kipling,
'The 'Eathen'

Two months before the British invasion, Lord Chelmsford had been introduced to the Boer leader Paul Kruger in Pietermaritzburg. Kruger, who had begun fighting Africans from the wagons of his childhood, contemplated the lankily-elegant, impeccably-mannered English general dourly, proffering blunt counsel: scout wide, he emphasised, to avoid being surprised by the fast-moving Zulu regiments, and always encamp in laager.

Chelmsford listened attentively. Considerate and tactful, if too withdrawn to appeal to the more extrovert settlers, he had heard a great deal of advice since arriving in South Africa, most of it from men whose precepts were based on frontier skirmishing in small bands, armed with flintlocks. If he suffered some of their views with private amusement, it was understandable. Few border farmers could envisage the scope of the projected operation, the power of its armaments, the professionalism of its personnel, its administrative resources and problems.

When Chelmsford had assumed command in March, the total British force bequeathed him had been a couple of artillery batteries, a company of engineers and half a dozen battalions, or part-battalions, of infantry – in all, about 5,000 troops. Now, as his army streamed into Zululand through the morning mists and swift-flowing rivers of January, it comprised almost 17,000 men with 725 carts and wagons, more than 7,600 draft oxen, mules and horses, 2,000,000 rounds of ammunition. Hundreds more commissariat wagons plied the lines of communication, watched over by a further eight companies of British infantry.

In the face of persistent governmental reluctance to provide reinforcements or finances, and the scattered reserves of the land itself, it represented a laborious and determined achievement. To supplement his British regulars, Chelmsford had drawn heavily on irregular units from the European colonists, part-time volunteers loosely organised as frontier and local defence vigilantes who, if their grand names – Royal Natal Carbineers, Royal Durban Rangers, Natal Hussars, etc. – belied their incorrigibly amateur character, were composed of expert horsemen and crack shots. Together with a number of quasi-military Natal police, these provided the general with over a thousand mounted men ideally qualified for scouting.

The other main source of local recruitment was Natal's Kaffir population, an element of the Bantu with little love for its neighbours in Zululand. Seven battalions of Kaffirs had been raised, each of 1,000 men, with European officers and NCOs, a significant portion of the force bearing firearms. Though sketchily trained and conspicuously erratic – the more circumspect of its officers contrived to be absent from shooting practice – the so-called Natal Native Contingent (NNC) was deemed more than equal to its numbers in native-led warriors.

At core, however, Chelmsford's confidence reposed in his British troops, more particularly the red-jacketed infantry of the line regiments, represented at the onset of the invasion by two battalions 24th, two battalions 90th, and single battalions 3rd, 4th, 13th and 99th. On top of these eight battalions, a ninth, the 80th Regiment, was held in reserve at Luneberg, on the Transvaal border. Each battalion comprised eight companies of ninety to a hundred men, plus officers, giving Chelmsford something approaching nine thousand professional soldiers of a calibre every loyal subject of the Empire (and some others) regarded as incomparable.

This had not always been so. Less than a century earlier, fresh from its humiliation in America, fossilised in ceremonial postures on the battlefield, too often deployed against hungry and frustrated demonstrators in England, the British army had been widely disparaged, even in Britain. The Crimea campaign had not enshrined its competence. Indeed, it was only in the last decade that Secretary for War Edward Cardwell's military reforms (outstandingly, the abolition of the sale of commissions) had produced the army's 'modern' reputation – and reduced his own, among the old-school die-hards, to infamy. Cardwell's overhaul, establishing the principle of promotion on merit, ending the recruitment of the socially rejected, and introducing new weapons, had greatly improved the image of the British soldier. He might not always succeed in the bizarre campaigns assigned to him, but at least he now had the wit and firepower to give a reasonable impression of doing so. Where the Georgian mobs had mustered to jeer him, Victorian crowds turned out to cheer him. It had become practically axiomatic that the returning hero was a conquering hero.

By and large, the British infantryman deserved the respect accorded him by friends and enemies. Bred lean and resourceful in the vicissitudes of survival among the chill grey slums of the industrial revolution, tempered in the flames of Burma, the Gold Coast and a score of Indian battlegrounds, the redcoat was a resilient, long-suffering fellow, often only too grateful to have escaped the dirt and unemployment of civilian life. The army was not concerned with his probable illiteracy and lack of accomplishment. It gave him a shilling a day (though most of it was kept back in 'stoppages'); it gave him regular food (if often only hardtack and corned beef); it gave him a sense of belonging, of companionship, in his regiment. Above all, it gave him a profession and the tools to compete in it.

Admittedly, the average officer was still a duffer, pushed into the army with a suitable remittance by an affluent family which regarded him deficient in the drive and intellect necessary to make a go of commercial or academic life. Supported by the system of social caste which effectively segregated them from the everyday rough and tumble of the other ranks – a somewhat distasteful business left to the ruder supervision of the NCOs – Her Majesty's officers yet clung to a cocooned world of servants, cigars and well-filled decanters, approaching campaigning abroad with the languid enthusiasm of an 'away' cricket fixture.

Tradition, however, was eroding. Cardwell's protégés, among them men who had risen on sheer merit from the bourgeoisie, were transforming the old command, providing the 'new school' of functional leadership their troops deserved. General Wolseley, figure-head of the *avant-garde*, himself the son of a Dublin shop-keeper, had actually published a treatise insisting that barrack-square drill was, by itself, not enough to fit soldiers for battle. A number of his disciples, a group scornfully dubbed the Wolseley Ring by traditionalists, was present in Chelmsford's force.

New school or old school – and Chelmsford appears to have fallen somewhere between camps – none believed in cosseting the rank and file. Amenities for the ordinary soldier varied from the crude, in barracks, to the non-existent on field service; the hazards from pox to malaria, to a spear in the abdomen. For the recalcitrant, there was the lash, or, in extremity, the hang-man's noose. But the average redcoat – moustachioed, unfrag-rant, an empire commuter in ammunition boots – seldom stepped out of line. Fighting was his business, and he took a pride in it.

The British soldier's best friend, though he cursed its mulish kick, was his rifle. Chelmsford's infantry, and many of his mounted men, were armed with the .45 Martini-Henry breech-loader, which, accurate up to a thousand yards, projected a heavy, soft-lead slug inflicting savage injuries. Each man normally carried seventy rounds in his ammunition pouches and knapsack. Extra ammuni-tion travelled with the battalion reserves, and a further stock with the expedition's supply trains. Battalion volley fire, opening at anything up to 800 yards, would deter the bravest enemy;

at 300 or 400 yards it was murderous. The average colonial settler had little idea of the havoc it could wreak on massed targets. The few hundred musket-armed Boers with whom Pretorius had routed the Zulu army ten years earlier would have regarded the expedition's firepower with amazement. Looking back to the outcome of Dingane's Day, Chelmsford had little logical cause for apprehension.

Nevertheless, he had paid some detailed attention to the enemy. In November he had published a report by his 'Intelligence Department' – compiled mainly by a seasoned border agent named Bernard Fynney, who had a penchant for collecting facts about Zulu arms – which was issued to officers for the invasion.

The Zulu army [ran this laconic document] is drawn from the entire male population, every male between the ages of sixteen and sixty-five being called upon to serve without exception. The military force (i.e., the effective field force) consists of fourteen corps or regiments divided into wings, right and left, and the latter into companies. These, however, are not of equal strength, but vary immensely, even from ten to two hundred (men), according to the numerical strength of the corps to which they belong. In fact, the companies and regiments would be more correctly termed families, or clans, and each corps possesses its own military headquarters, or kraal, with the following hierarchy: namely, one commanding officer, chief, or Induna-Yesibaya; one second-in-command, major, or Induna-Yohlangoti, who has charge of the left wing; two wing and company officers, according to the need of the battalion. As a rule, all these officers have command of men the same age as themselves, and the method of recruiting is as follows:

At stated and periodical intervals, usually from two to five years, a general levy takes place, when all the youths who happen at the time to have attained the age of fifteen are formed into a regiment and undergo a year's probation, during which time they are supposed to pass from boyhood to manhood. As the regiment becomes disciplined and seasoned, it receives large drafts from other corps, so that as the elders die out young men come in to fill the ranks. The entire Zulu army consists of thirty-three regiments, married or unmarried. No one in Zululand, male or female, is allowed to marry without the king's permission, and this is never granted till the men are forty years of age.* Then they have to shave the crown of the head, put a ring round it, and carry a white shield, in contradistinction to the unmarried regiments, who do not shave their heads, and who carry coloured shields. Many of these regiments are too young for active service, others are too old ...

We have heard a great deal about the drill of these, but their movements, so far as we can learn, are few and very simple, but very quickly performed in their own way. They form circles of regiments in order to outflank the enemy. From this formation they break into columns of regiments, or companies, and from these into skirmishing order, with supports and reserves. The sole commissariat of the Zulu army consists of three or four days' grain, carried by the lads who follow each corps, and, if necessary, of a herd of cattle driven with each column.

In many ways, the information filtered to Chelmsford about the Zulu army contained an unconscious strain of parody. Militarily, this small black nation, these 'heathen savages', curiously echoed the martial fabric of the white imperialists. Like his British counterpart, the Zulu warrior had been reared on the illusion of supremacy, of national invincibility. Like the imperial redcoat, the Zulu nurtured an intense pride of regiment, a tradition of courage and resilience, an iron code of discipline. In both forces, for instance, overt cowardice and the rape of women, enemy or otherwise, called for capital punishment.

Like the heroes of Victoria's empire, the Zulu soldier was a phlegmatic, articulate fellow with a native wit which belied his illiteracy. (Nineteen thousand Zulu words were recorded in the last century, a vocabulary not far short of Shakespeare's.) Even in their attitudes to celibacy, the authorities of white empress and black king were remarkably similar. Asked why his soldiers had to wait to marry, Shaka had once replied: 'Marriage for young warriors is folly. Their first and last duty is to protect the interests of the nation. This they cannot do efficiently if they have family ties.' British War Office policy, favouring the recruit-

---

* In fact, it *was* granted earlier, sometimes as an individual reward, occasionally to an entire regiment in token of meritorious service – Author.

ment of unmarried men, might have been defined identically. Though Zulu morality, as that of Victorian England, was strict on sexual matters, some latitude was condoned, if only tacitly, in the behaviour of the soldiery of both sides. As Kipling put it for the Queen's men:

> We aren't no thin red 'eroes, nor we aren't no blackguards too,
> But single men in barricks, most remarkable like you;
> An' if sometimes our conduck isn't all your fancy paints,
> Why, single men in barricks don't grow into plaster saints.

While the British soldier relieved his frustration with the whores of the Empire, the unmarried Zulu, lacking brothels or prostitutes, had to seek accommodation with respectable single girls. Since the deflowering of a Zulu maiden would have been a social disaster, her pregnancy a worse one, bachelor warriors became adept at a sexual technique, *uku-hlobonga*, limiting phallic penetration to the labia majora, minora and fourchette. Ejaculation took place in the perineum, the female keeping her thighs locked, at the same time synchronising her orgasm. Intercourse after battle, to *sula izembe*, or wipe the axe, was an old tradition in the regiments.

So was the award of decorations for bravery in combat. Warriors who had distinguished themselves in battle earned the right to wear brilliant feathers, as the British wore medals. Successful Zulu commanders received honours and riches, as did British generals. Wolseley had received a personal grant of £25,000 after his last campaign. Zulu indunas had been awarded up to five hundred head of cattle after victories.

But of all characteristics, perhaps none linked the Zulu warrior so closely in spirit with the Victorian redcoat as his readiness to advance regardless of danger. Defence is a natural posture – history abounds in epic defensive actions – but the willingness to advance into high risk from a position of security, to defy the instinct of survival, is rarer, a perversion of nature much prized by generals. The Zulu traditionally fought going forward. It was, as Chelmsford knew, a conditional military asset. Combined with superior equipment, insistent bravery was the irresistible attribute;

combined with inferior equipment, it could bring disaster. On this, he based his calculations. The equation was a simple one: the firepower of his line regiments, plus the headlong courage of a naked enemy, equalled the destruction of Cetshwayo's host. Like lemmings, the Zulus would destroy themselves in their stubborn rush.

The British army of invasion entered Zululand by three of the four main border trails. The right column, under Colonel Charles Pearson of the 3rd East Kent, an officer who had been prominent at the siege of Sebastopol, crossed at the Lower Drift of the Tugela, on the coastal plain, to strike north by way of an old mission station at Eshowe. The centre column, under Colonel Richard Glyn of the 2nd battalion, another Crimea veteran, crossed at Rorke's Drift, on the Buffalo, some eighty miles inland, thrusting east. The left column, commanded by Perthshire's Colonel Evelyn Wood, a Wolseley adherent of wide experience, struck south-east from the disputed northern territories across the headwaters of the Blood River, a tributary of the Buffalo. A reserve column, mainly of levies under Colonel Anthony Durnford, Royal Engineers, a former assistant commissioner of roads in Ceylon, waited at the fourth crossing, the Middle Drift, about halfway between Lower Drift and Rorke's Drift.

The three advancing columns were to converge, maintaining cohesion through flank communications, on Cetshwayo's capital of Ulundi. By this strategy, Chelmsford sought to impress his strength on as much of the kingdom as possible, to screen the border from any attempt at counter-invasion, and, most importantly, to ensure that the Zulu army attacked him.

To have advanced in a single mass, it was reasoned, might have deterred even the Zulu generals from confrontation. With the entire country in which to disperse, Cetshwayo's regiments could have awaited a British withdrawal with impunity, then emerged as strong as ever. Ulundi might be burned, and a few other dwelling sites, but the domed wattle-and-thatch huts of the Zulus could quickly be rebuilt. The futility of the single-column punitive expedition had been proved in too many parts of the Empire. If the Zulu army was to be invited to impale itself, it was more likely to be on one of Chelmsford's three prongs than on a single massively invulnerable skewer.

As the British general watched his wagons labouring across the undulating, rock-strewn frontier, his chief worry – ironically, as it turned out – was that the clash would not come soon enough. The long, cumbersome vehicles, with their creaking wooden wheels and teams of lugubrious oxen, were the crux of his anxiety.

With every other adjunct of warfare in his favour, Chelmsford was burdened with the inevitable drawback of the 'modern' army : the sheer weight of its essential supplies and equipment. Each battalion consumed a ton or more of food a day, perhaps a ton and a half of fuel, and required at least nine tons of camp equipment. On top of which there were field guns, ordnance supplies, kitchens, medical stores, engineering, signalling and farriers' equipment, animal fodder, and so on. At a rough estimate, the invasion forces would have to shift 2,500 tons of supplies and hardware for every week it remained in Zululand, and since this involved not only the transport with the columns, but a relay of supply trains, the problem would increase as the columns advanced.

In the final analysis, to Chelmsford's inescapable frustration, the progress of his most sophisticated armaments depended on a very unsophisticated animal, the ox, thousands of which were harnessed to his wagons in teams of from eight to eighteen animals.

As a form of tractive power, the ox team had a number of drawbacks. Though capable of hauling a ton at three miles an hour on good roads (hardly a feature of Zululand), it spent an inordinate proportion of each day refuelling. Of every twenty-four hours, eight had to be allowed for grazing, eight for chewing cud, and another two for resting in the midst of its exertions. In the remaining six, a poor track, or soft ground, might limit progress to a mere mile or two. An awkward stream or ridge could well take a day to cross. The security problem posed by these straggling, slow-moving trains was considerable. Thirty fully spanned wagons in column would stretch a mile, a vulnerable target demanding the protection of many troops who could otherwise have been deployed clearing ground ahead.

In all, the consequences were anomalous. While Cetshwayo's barefoot impis could have marched from the Tugela to Ulundi in two days, Chelmsford, with some of the best-equipped troops in the world, could not guarantee to camp his army there in under two weeks, even unopposed. Allowing for opposition, he calculated on a minimum of six weeks' campaigning, and a likelihood that he would not be through within two months. The consensus of the regular ranks was with him in hoping for an early action. The sooner the Zulu army appeared, the quicker it could be dealt with and the campaign concluded.

To this end, the first natives captured by Chelmsford within Zululand, an isolated group of unarmed cattle herders, were carefully rehearsed in the scope of the invasion then turned loose to transmit the news to Ulundi. By the somewhat novel process of providing the enemy with accurate, first-hand intelligence, Chelmsford hoped to curtail the delay he imagined must occur before the king could muster his regiments. In this lay the first miscalculation.

Chelmsford's headquarters was with the centre column, which had commenced the crossing at Rorke's Drift on 11 January, at two in the morning, with what the special correspondent for the London *Standard*, an ex-army man named Charles Norris-Newman, regarded as inconsiderable complications. A quantity of cigars and gin had been stolen from the officers' baggage in the night. A number of troops lost their way in the dank mist. Several men of a NNC battalion were swept off in the river and drowned. But these were accounted minor details – with the possible exception of the gin, which provoked a fruitless inquiry. The British infantry and transport was ferried safely in pontoons.

The crossing was scarcely complete when Chelmsford received word from Durnford, commanding the reserves at Middle Drift, that a Zulu attack on Natal was rumoured, in consequence of which he intended moving his men to a new defensive position. Durnford, a rather supercilious-looking man with a beaver moustache, receding hair and a disabled left arm, had taken to a fighting command with impulsive enthusiasm. After years of surveying roads, his new command, albeit of native troops, had quickened the soldier in him, and he had lost no time in seizing an initiative. Chelmsford received his news in pained silence.

> Dear Durnford [he replied frigidly], Unless you carry out the instructions I give you, it will be my unpleasant duty to remove you from your command, and to substitute another officer ... You have simply received information which may or may not be true and which you have no means of verifying. If movements ordered are to be delayed because report hints at a chance of an invasion of Natal, it will be impossible for me to carry out my plan of campaign. I trust you will understand this plain speaking and not give me any further occasion to write in a style which is distasteful to me.

The distaste was not affected. It was alien to Chelmsford's reserve to vent his feelings, to allow the tall, colourless, patriarchal shell of the general to be ruffled by the inner man. 'I do not,' he had once written, 'let the outside world penetrate into my secret thoughts.' Durnford's impulsiveness worried him. Though the matter was closed to further comment, Chelmsford subsequently shifted the colonel's posting to Rorke's Drift, where he might more readily be supervised.

Meanwhile, the centre column slowly uncoiled from the congested camp area and, under a hot sun offset by the bracing altitude, struck east along the overgrown ruts of some old trading wagons. Richard Glyn, the column commander, was a short, testy man who compensated for his lack of height by his contentiousness. In both physique and temperament, he was the antithesis of Chelmsford – a sort of Pancho to Quixote – and, riding stirrup to stirrup, they made an odd pair. The steel of the column reposed in the 1st and 2nd battalions of Glyn's own regiment, the 24th Foot (later the South Wales Borderers), now sustaining an historical connection with South Africa based on its original participation in the capture of Capetown. The 24th wore bright green facings on their red jackets and, like all the regular units, the regimental badge on their sun helmets.

1. With the Natal Native Contingent: Cooking Breakfast in an Ant Heap Oven.—2. Wounded Refugees Seeking Protection at an English Camp.—3. 1 p.m. "Dinner."—4. The Zulu Ceremony, "Gia," or "Defiance to the Enemy."—5. With the Natal Native Contingent: Punishment Parade—Flogging a Deserter.—6. At Bay: "We are Soldiers. We've Shown You how We can Fight, and I'll Show You how We can Die."

Illustration from *The Graphic*, 5 April 1879. Captions read: 1 With the Natal Native Contingent: Cooking Breakfast in an Ant Heap Oven 2 Wounded Refugees Seeking Protection at an English Camp 3 1 p.m. 'Dinner' 4 The Zulu Ceremony 'Gia,' or 'Defiance to the Enemy' 5 With the Natal Native Contingent: Punishment Parade—Flogging a Deserter 6 At Bay: 'We are Soldiers. We've shown You how We can Fight and I'll Show You how We can Die.'

The Radio Times Hulton Picture Library

An uncommon portrait by F. Sargent showing
Lord Chelmsford without his beard.
The National Portrait Gallery, London

Lord Chelmsford and his staff, January 1879.
Standing: Major M. Gosset, Lieut. A. Berkeley
Milne, R.N. *Seated*: Cdr. H. J. F. Campbell,
Lord Chelmsford, Lieut.-Col. J. North Crealock.
The Killie Campbell Africana Library, Durban

Top Dabulamanzi, standing centre, and warriors.
The Killie Campbell Africana Library, *Durban*

Bottom Gatling gun and limber used during the
Zulu War.
The National Army Museum

Zulu warrior in full regalia, from an early print.
The South African Government Archives

A young Zulu warrior in war dress.
The National Army Museum

Sir Garnet Wolseley, 1880. Painting by Besnard.
The National Portrait Gallery, London

Top The Battle of Isandhlwana. Oil painting by
C. E. Fripp.
The National Army Museum

Bottom Lord Chelmsford's retreat from
Isandhlwana. An artist's impression taken from
The Graphic, 29 March 1879.
The Radio Times Hulton Picture Library

Heading the column's mounted strength were a hundred or more troopers of the Natal Mounted Police under John Dartnell, a former imperial officer who had sold out his commission to take up farming in South Africa. Turning to police work, Dartnell had slogged hard to shape a scruffy, poorly-endowed force into a useful outfit. Recruited both from Britain and the colony, it comprised hardy, well-trained men accustomed to operating individually or in groups. Whatever attracted them to the job, it was not money. From their modest pay they were normally obliged to provide their own uniforms and keep, buy their horses and equipment and purchase forage. The expedition to Zululand came as a break to them. With the army issuing rations and fodder, they had never been so well off.

Supplementing the mounted police was a body of irregular cavalry, about 120 strong, including contingents of the Natal Carbineers, the Buffalo Border Guard and the Newcastle Rifles – self-supporting territorial units composed largely of landed settlers. Ostensibly local defence vigilantes, there had been little prior call on their services. In ordinary circumstances, they met periodically to drink, gossip and indulge in not-too-strenuous drill sessions under their elected officers, who included two Shepstones, sons of Theophilus.

Completing the fighting strength of the centre column were N battery, 5th brigade, Royal Artillery, commanded by a dependable if prosaic Major Arthur Harness, the middle-aged bachelor son of a retired general, and a regiment of the NNC under a plump but energetic young commander, Rupert de la Tour Lonsdale, late of the 74th Highlanders. Lonsdale had acquired a bright reputation leading levies against recalcitrant tribesmen, but was feeling less than bright at the moment, having fallen from his pony and not yet fully recovered from concussion. He was still ailing when his subordinates sampled the first action of the campaign.

Chelmsford's wagons had scarcely started rolling when the leaders were bogged down in marshland, and the engineers were called on to improvise a causeway. While this was in hand, the general resolved on a dawn sally against a kraal of the Sirayo clan, which lay in a valley a few miles ahead. The raid was to be led by Lonsdale's levies, supported by four companies of the 24th, and covered by cavalry. Chelmsford and his staff went along to observe a curtain-raiser as undemanding as it was un-provoked.

During the advance on the valley, a small party of Zulu herds-men, hastily rounding up their cattle, raised the alarm in the quiet kraal. Sirayo, and many of his men, were at Ulundi for the First Fruits Festival. Some of those who remained resolutely took station on the rocky approaches to their commune, demand-ing by what authority the soldiers threatened them. 'By the orders of the great white queen!' exclaimed a loud voice. Where-upon a volley of rocks descended without ceremony on the great white queen's representatives, while ragged musket fire spluttered from the steep slopes.

Though the Zulus still fought mainly with their assegais, a quantity of firearms had been imported since Dingane's time, conspicuously from Birmingham, whose arms factories had never been slow to shake a profit from any side in Britain's colonial conflicts. For the most part, however – since patriotism could not entirely be discounted, and Britain's tribal enemies were not rich – the guns supplied to the Africans were 'cheap, nasty and obsolete', less likely to harm those at whom they were aimed, in many cases, than those who aimed them.

Nevertheless, the Kaffir levies now wavered. This was predict-able. Experience elsewhere in Africa had shown that while native allies would put up with a lot in return for the trifling hand-outs and dubious promises of the European, they weighed the bargain more carefully when bullets started flying. The normal white response came in two alternatives: 1) they were driven with threats and buffetings from behind, or 2) they were shamed by disdainful leadership at the front. These alternatives were per-sonified in Lonsdale's force by a rugged Irish commander named Hamilton Browne, whose crude methods had done much to dis-enchant the levies, and by Henry Harford, a fresh-faced lieutenant seconded to the NNC because he spoke Bantu. While Browne swore and lashed at the faltering Kaffirs, Harford galumphed forward flourishing a rifle and encouraging them in their own tongue.

In his enthusiasm, he ran straight into the muzzle of a Zulu musket. The Zulu pulled the trigger. To Harford's intense relief, the antiquated weapon failed to fire. The mêlée which ensued was a short one. Advancing from the rear at a brisk jog, the British infantry drove both the levies and the Zulu defenders before them. It was over by breakfast. Several dozen Zulus were killed or captured, Sirayo's kraal was burned and a thousand head of livestock – the clan's subsistence – driven off to the British lines. Among the dead was Nkumbikazulu, a son of the absent chief, who had stood bravely against the unexpected spoilers. Since Frere had named his family among the causes of the invasion, this was regarded by Chelmsford's staff as rough justice. A number of women and children taken, including Sirayo's eldest wife and a daughter, were turned loose on the general's orders to return to their ravaged community. The Zulu people had had a foretaste of what to expect from the invaders.

Chapter Four

A
LIKELY
SPOT

ఆఴఴఴఴ

Uya kuhlasela-pi na?
He! Uya kuhlasela-pi na?

Where will you make war?
Yes! Where will you make war?

Chant attributed to Shaka's warriors.

THE British assumption that Cetshwayo would need time to marshal his warriors from the districts implied ignorance of one of the major events of the Zulu calendar. For all its detailed analysis of the Zulu army, Chelmsford's intelligence department had overlooked the First Fruits Festival. The king's council might dispute the method of deploying its armed force, but, altogether fortuitously, the regiments were at Ulundi, ready to move off.

While the invaders ferried the frontier, more than 20,000 warriors, in twelve regiments – from the youthful uVe, recently formed by Cetshwayo, to the veteran umKhulutshane, whose men were well into their sixties – awaited orders at Nodwengu kraal, the great central barracks near the royal court. Thick-necked, broad of shoulder and thigh, they displayed their war regalia doughtily: vivid bird plumes, fur loin strips, fronded bands on legs strong from the peripatetic life. Their brightly daubed oval shields, each large enough to screen a crouching man, were of ox hide stretched on a wooden frame.

Those who had firearms disported them awkwardly. The Zulu was no marksman. His customary weapon was the assegai, which he wielded as deftly as a *garde-manger* wields a carving knife. From childhood, such games as *uku gwaza insema* (stabbing the insema, a ball-like tuber, with sharpened sticks) and mock duelling had conditioned his reflexes; later, the hunting field trained him more seriously. Soon after pubescence (*uku-tomba*), probably about the age of fifteen, the youthful Zulu became liable, with the rest of his age-group, to conscription. Leaving the homestead, he would then present himself at a military kraal for initiation and apprenticeship, eventually being drafted to a regiment of his generation. The enlisted Zulu was more than just a soldier. He was a member of the state construction force, repairing and building kraals and barracks; he was a policeman, employed to arrest offenders or deal with the convicted; he was a guardian of the royal herds, among other national property, and a craftsman manufacturing shields and assegais.

Zulu smelters extracted the metal for their spearheads from laterite, a ferruginous local rock handily crumbled into the small clay furnaces which were usually charged with a mixture of ore and charcoal. The long blade of the stabbing assegai, slightly fluted and honed until razor-sharp, was forged with a pointed shank to fit the short hardwood shaft, into which it was glued with the juice of a bulbous root (*scilla rigidifolia*). The haft was then bound around the impaled shank with fresh ox skin which, as it dried and shrank, provided a perfect finish to the fixture.

With no wage, and little keep, the Zulu warrior maintained himself principally on gifts from home and the innate hospitality of the community at large, performing his chores with good humour, comradeship and a natural sense of discipline which called for little supervision. As a fundamental of society, the Zulu deferred to age and experience, but functional capacity was also recognised, and in matters of military leadership the elderly shared responsibility with relatively young men.

As the senior member of Cetshwayo's council, Mnyamana, a sexagenarian induna virtually holding the position of prime minister, had an influential voice in war policy, but gave way in the field to a supreme command of two chiefs separated in age by more than thirty years. Tshingwayo was a spirited veteran in his seventies. While reluctantly conceding his inability to wield a spear with his former vigour, he still marched with the regiments. Half a century of soldiering backed his reputation for tactical acumen and aggression.

His co-general, Mavumengwana, a mere forty years of age, had been promoted from command of the uThulwana, a regiment originally created by Mpande and in which Cetshwayo had once served. The leadership of the uThulwana now belonged to the king's younger brother, Dabulamanzi, a stockily-handsome thirty-five-year-old of panache and precipitation. The uThulwana regiment was kraal'd with another, the uDloko, at Undi, the second big military base which, with Nodwengu, provided perhaps the two strongest components of the Zulu army. Dabulamanzi assumed overall command of the Undi force.

Among the commanders of the young regiments, a couple may be mentioned as representative of divergent attitudes in the Zulu middle leadership. Sigcwelegcwele, strong-headed and bellicose, spoiled for a fight at the head of the inGobamakhosi regiment. A year before, he had led his warriors in a brawl with the older uThulwana regiment, a rumpus ending in serious fighting and many deaths. On the other hand, Usibebu, commander of the inDlu-Yengwe, a man higher in the king's esteem, stood for restraint and diplomacy. Usibebu had been among those to advocate cautious investigation of Frere's ultimatum with a view to preserving peace. Now, out-voted by the majority, he prepared for battle.

Regimental custom called for bulls to be driven into the barracks, their necks broken and parts of their intestines mixed with herbs in a brew administered by the witch-doctors as a war beverage and anointment. The remainder of the animals was then roasted and pieces of flesh tossed to the assembled troops, who scrambled for what might well prove the bulk of their protein for the campaign.

It is difficult, in the absence of written records of the Zulu council, to be precise about Cetshwayo's handling of the invasion crisis. His own testimony is one of shock and confusion. 'My father was a great friend of the English,' he said later. 'I was a great friend of the English nation, and thought I would reign and die at peace with the English. I know not why they sought to punish me. Nobody can come before my face and prove that I did any wrong to the English.' According to the South African correspondent of the London *Morning Post*, the king's sole aim was the defence of his kingdom. 'The Zulu king never attempted an invasion of British territory, but stood on the defensive even after we attacked his country.'

This is borne out by Zulu tradition, which stresses Cetshwayo's order that his army should in no circumstances engage the British beyond the boundary of Zululand. He seems to have clung to the despairing hope, even by mid-January, that the British might still have second thoughts and go away.

Such of Cetshwayo's instructions as survived in oral annals scarcely suggest the militaristic ogre Frere painted. Neither dramatic exhortation nor dynamic scheming are recorded – simply the rather mundane guidance to his captains that the British soldiers could be spotted by their red coats, that any attack should be in daylight (a strangely ill-advised stricture) and that the army should march slowly, ostensibly to conserve energy, though not improbably with the idea that somehow Providence might yet intervene. It was enough for the warriors. The response to a royal command was unwavering: 'U-Zulu! U-Qobolwayo! Nkosi yama Kosi! Bayete! The Zulu! Their very essence! Hail King of Kings! Thy will be done!' Late on 17 January, the regiments marched from Nodwengu, heading west.

The same day, Chelmsford rode east from Rorke's Drift to fix a site for his next camp. The engineers had completed their roadworks, and he was ready to move ahead. Ten miles into Zululand, he found an adequately-watered spot, well provided with fuel wood. On the 20th, bands playing, brass gleaming on jolting artillery, the column marched up to it. A mile or two to the right of the line of advance, the Buffalo swirled on a parallel course back to the crossing point. Closer to the left, the ground rose steeply to a lofty range, the Nqutu. Rounding the southwestern corner of this, the vanguard crossed a small donga, or gully, continued a mile or so in the southern shadow of the Nqutu, then was faced starkly by a craggy spur, or leg, jutting across its path from the larger mass. At the foot of the spur, separated by a humped pass, stood a tall, stony outcrop, or kopje.

As the leaders rode through the humped pass, they swung left, under the far face of the spur, and halted. This was the camp site – Isandhlwana. In many respects it seemed excellent. On high, dry ground, the force would have its back to the rugged wall of the spur, with the sharp escarpment of the Nqutu plateau on its left. To its front, looking east towards Ulundi, a wide plain, laced with forking rivulets, stretched some eight or nine miles to a series of hills, the Nkandhla and Isipezi. On the southern border of the plain, facing the Nqutu across perhaps six miles of flat veld, stood another range incorporating the heights of Malakatas and Inhlazatye.

An enemy approaching across the plain would be spotted miles away; pickets atop the Nqutu escarpment would have a fair view of the northern plateau. The troops moved in efficiently.

Close behind the vanguard, Lonsdale and his two battalions of levies wheeled off the track and followed the spur face towards the Nqutu escarpment to form the northernmost wing of the new camp. Aligned at orderly intervals in front of the spur, looking back from Lonsdale's tents to the track, were the 2nd battalion of the 24th, then Harness and his artillery, followed by the mounted contingent and finally, across the track and nearest the outlying kopje, the 1st battalion of the 24th. Tucked in the narrow space between this line and the spur were the column command post and the tents of Chelmsford's staff.

Two aspects of Chelmsford's generalship, already discernible in the preamble to Isandhlwana, now crystallised. The first was his preoccupation with the centre column. That the general's need to supervise the overall progress of his three-pronged advance was best facilitated by attaching his headquarters to the mediate station followed logically. That he should usurp the function of the commander of that column to some extent was less fortunate. Glyn's position had already begun to look ambiguous. With each day that passed, he seemed more like the second-in-command of the column than its commanding officer. Chelmsford's increasing intervention in tactics and routine dispositions was not calculated to produce the best from the touchy colonel. Nor, for that matter, did the involvement of the general's staff in such matters do anything to clarify the chain of command and transmission of orders. Indeed, the resulting blurring of hierarchic status was to lead to open confusion very shortly.

The second aspect, compounding the implications of the first, was the disparity between Chelmsford's published instructions for the campaign and his personal leadership. Pre-eminent among the detailed regulations issued to his commanders prior to the invasion had been specific orders for laagering or entrenching at all field camps, which he clearly proposed should be strongly defensible. Had Chelmsford not been present with the column, Glyn could scarcely have overlooked such orders, yet no laagering or entrenching had been attempted since the force entered Zululand. The lines at Isandhlwana stretched for nearly half a mile without a trench or a barrier in front of them.

Of course, there were problems, especially in laagering. Of the ponderous wagons which had started for the new camp on the 20th, almost a third had failed to arrive by dusk. Detachments of infantry had to stand guard over stranded vehicles, some up to their loading boards in boggy spruits, on the open trail overnight. Those which had turned up were marshalled in a sprawling mass in the humped pass, between spur and kopje, with their own guard. To stipulate laagering was one thing – to manoeuvre unwieldy vehicles, with weary teams, at the end of a day's trek was another. Yet the other columns were doing it, the Boer settlers had done it, and Kruger had proclaimed it an essential priority.

Chelmsford's neglect to heed Kruger – more oddly, to heed his own orders – discomfited some officers, notably the colonials. Others made light of it. Boer tactics, they pointed out, had been based on the need for small, modestly-armed parties to survive against heavy odds. Now the boot was on the other foot. Building barriers would not merely be pointless, but a positive hindrance. The need was to press on, to get to grips, to get the job done. The raid on Sirayo's kraal had raised a false measure of Zulu force. When Sirayo's brother, Gamdana – a local patriarch, albeit an ailing, feebly supported one – came in to surrender, the optimists were sustained. Chelmsford, they agreed, was playing his hand right. He had patrols out, vedettes on Nqutu, a picket line on the plain. The only defensive system required was a warning to alert the camp. The red lines of British infantry would do the rest.

On the afternoon of the 20th, Chelmsford rode the length of the plain towards Ulundi and examined the Nkandhla hills without seeing any Zulus. As he could not be sure, however, that the Nkandhla, or the hills to the south of the plain, were not screening a hostile force, he issued instructions that evening for a thorough search on the 21st. At first light in the morning, two groups set out to accomplish this task. One, a compact posse of some 150 horsemen of the Natal police and irregulars, took the easterly course to the Nkandhla. They were led by Dartnell of the NMP, who, as the only professional mounted commander present, had been placed in charge of the entire column cavalry.

The other force, ranging forth in more straggling fashion, comprised the best part of the native contingent, under Lonsdale. Lonsdale's instructions were to strike south to the Malakatas, then work east along the range to join Dartnell. Though conspicuously overweight, and still not fully fit, Lonsdale plunged into the southern hills with an enthusiasm unshared by his Kaffirs or his diminutive and long-suffering pony, the mare Dot. About ten hours later, he emerged with an exhausted, foot-sore following and little to show for his labours save a herd of captured cattle, which he despatched to Isandhlwana while his men rested.

From a couple of unarmed Zulus he had captured in the hills, the heavy-handed Browne had beaten the information that Cetshwayo's army had mustered many days ago and was now probably on its way to intercept Chelmsford. All that the Kaffirs and their European NCOs (a rough lot, recruited from the poor end of the colonial community) now wanted was to get back to camp and eat. The natives, fed once a day, had tasted no food for more than twenty-four hours, and had no rations with them. But Lonsdale, still three miles short of the Nkandhla, had yet to link with Dartnell, as ordered. He now sent young Harford ahead to make contact.

Harford returned with unpalatable news for the levies. Dartnell's horsemen had located several hundred Zulus in the eastern hills. Since the hour was late, he had decided, contrary to instructions, not to return to camp that night, but to stay where he was and seek Chelmsford's permission to attack in the morning. He asked Lonsdale to join him.

Lonsdale's officers opposed the scheme vehemently. To expect men, already weary and famished, to spend the chill night in the hills without food or cover was one thing, as Browne declaimed robustly – to expect them to fight next morning was another. When Lonsdale, impervious to argument, heaved himself aboard his pony, resolved to join Dartnell, several of his officers and NCOs turned about in disgust and made tracks for camp on their own account. The remainder moved on towards the cavalry and a restless night on the eastern slopes, where Browne and his fellow Europeans maintained a semblance of discipline by relieving the panicky Kaffirs of their firearms and bludgeoning them into huddled groups.

Chelmsford had visited the vedettes above camp, on the Nqutu escarpment, that afternoon. While he was with them, a party of about a dozen Zulus appeared on a ridge perhaps a mile away, spotted the vedettes and disappeared. It was, Chelmsford learned from his mounted lookouts, the first sign of enemy activity on the plateau to date. He was returning to camp when Dartnell's intention to stay out on the Nkandhla was conveyed to him, together with a request for reinforcements. He refused the request. Like Durnford before, Dartnell had exceeded his authority, and the general's undemonstrative nature did not wholly conceal his annoyance. The reconnaissance forces had been given clear orders to return in daylight. It was now too late to recall them before nightfall. Instead, he ordered blankets and sustenance to be sent by pack-horse to the aggravating Dartnell.

If Chelmsford turned in with a grievance that evening, he had not long to dwell on it. At 1.30 in the morning, he was roused by a second message from the Nkandhla. The bearer had left Dartnell's position before dusk but, overtaken by darkness, had found difficulty picking his way across the broad plain. His news was significant. The few hundred Zulus reported earlier had been heavily augmented. Dartnell's men had eventually observed an estimated 2,000 warriors in the Isipezi region of the eastern hills. Taken with hints already received of a large-scale Zulu advance from Ulundi, the implications were not obscure. At least part of Cetshwayo's army was approaching the head of the plain. Isandhlwana had to be regarded as its probable target.

On the face of it, it was what Chelmsford wanted. He had picked Isandhlwana on its merits as a battleground. All his transport was off the trail. The main strength of the column, the imperial infantry and artillery, was at readiness, fed and resting, with ample time to prepare for what, at earliest, would be an attack in the morning. The general was lucky. He might have been caught on the march – or pitching or striking camp.

Only the waywardness of Dartnell and Lonsdale spoiled the picture. With some 1,600 men between them, overwhelmingly Natal natives, they could hardly oppose the Zulu army if it approached them in full strength. However, since none was better placed to appraise the danger, and since the capacity of both commanders to act independently of orders had been all too well evidenced, they might be relied upon to withdraw with alacrity. Indeed, had they considered themselves in any way imperilled, presumably the entire force would have returned to camp that night instead of just a messenger. They were, after all, unencumbered and highly mobile.

On such a reckoning, Chelmsford's decision, as he now pondered Dartnell's report by candlelight, was an odd one. By any reckoning, the details of its implementation were peculiar.

Having earlier refused Dartnell modest reinforcement, Chelmsford now resolved to reinforce him urgently and in no uncertain manner: namely, with six of the twelve imperial infantry battalions at Isandhlwana, and four of the six guns in the artillery battery. In other words, considered briefly, he intended to take almost half the strength from the camp and march it ten miles to an unsurveyed and unprepared position to face an enemy of uncertain numbers who might well, by the time the force arrived, be somewhere else – not unreasonably at Isandhlwana. Furthermore, Chelmsford not only decided to place Glyn in charge of this relief force, but to join Dartnell himself, thus depriving the camp of its two senior officers.

Whether Chelmsford's primary impulse in this extraordinary nocturnal decision was to save Dartnell and Lonsdale from some imagined calamity, or a sudden urge to take the tactical offensive, is uncertain. What emerges clearly from the hustle surrounding the departure is the precipitance with which the general transmitted his intentions to a surprised camp, largely through the medium of his military secretary, Lieutenant-Colonel John Crealock.

The officer left in charge at Islandhlwana, Lieutenant-Colonel Henry Pulleine of the 1st battalion 24th, never saw Chelmsford before the march-out, only learning of his new responsibility at second-hand. At 2 am, on the general's instructions, Crealock addressed a cryptic message to Durnford, at Rorke's Drift, ordering him to move up 'at once' with his reserves to reinforce Pulleine. 'The General and Colonel Glyn move off at once to attack a Zulu force about ten miles distant,' added Crealock. It was not until well after Chelmsford's departure from camp that he thought to inquire of his secretary the precise orders he had left at Isandhlwana.

Glyn, with the 2nd battalion of the 24th, and Harness with his hastily assembled gun teams, followed Chelmsford onto the dim plain at 3.30 am, and headed east towards the Nkandhla. Seven hours later, when Durnford rode in from Rorke's Drift with his native reserves, Pulleine had his men standing-by in a thin line before the depleted camp, wide gaps where the 2nd battalion of the 24th and two thirds of the artillery had once been. Durnford and Pulleine shook hands somewhat cagily, the latter observing that his vedettes had reported Zulu activity on the Nqutu plateau. Durnford was senior to Pulleine (substantively a major) both in rank and intellectual pretension, and though Pulleine had been left in charge at the time of the general's departure, it could be argued that the camp command now devolved on the engineer. Unfortunately, Chelmsford, in his haste, had not clarified the matter. When Durnford tested the issue by asking for a couple of companies of the 24th to join his reserves in a probe beyond the outposts, Pulleine stuck his toes in. He was a no-nonsense veteran of twenty-four years' service, and not impressed by a superior attitude. As far as Pulleine was concerned, he had been entrusted with the defence of the camp and had no intention of handing his infantry over to a sapper.

According to the contemporary authors of *The Story of the Zulu Campaign*, 'he declined, saying his orders were to guard the camp, and he could not, under the circumstances, let them go without a positive command'. Durnford let it drop. The protocol remained in limbo.

Across the plain, on the eastern hills, Dartnell and Lonsdale welcomed the dawn with gratitude. It had been a cold night, the small quantity of provisions sent from camp had not extended to the miserable Kaffirs, and, on more than one occasion, mass desertions had threatened in the darkness. For Lonsdale's officers, seeking to control the restless levies, the Zulu had seemed the least of their problems. Morning consolidated this viewpoint, for, far from revealing the enemy army, it produced merely the embarrassment of Lord Chelmsford, who had spurred on ahead of Glyn and his main force. When Dartnell recovered from his astonishment at finding half the camp moving to support him, he was compelled to report that the Zulus had disappeared.

In some frustration, Chelmsford now sent orders to Glyn to work the advancing infantry and guns to the north of Dartnell and start searching for the enemy. Soon after, the general rode to join them. Whereupon, with excruciating perversity, a substantial Zulu war-party appeared on a ridge ahead of Dartnell and Lonsdale.

Inspired to redeem themselves, Lonsdale chivvied his battalions forward while Dartnell detoured the ridge with his cavalry and hovered in the vale behind. As the Zulus retired before the out-numbering levies, the mounted men pounced on them, dispersing the warriors and inflicting many casualties. In the skirmish which followed, the agile Harford pursued three Zulus into a cleft in the hillside, killing two and detaining the other. By the time Chelmsford and Glyn arrived with the British troops, the bulk of the remaining enemy were dead ones, their compatriots hav-ing melted south-east across the Mangeni – a tributary of the Buffalo skirting the range to the south of the plain and tailing up behind the eastern heights.

Chelmsford, having combed the hills at the head of the plain without sighting Cetshwayo's army, was now forced to take stock. The band Dartnell and Lonsdale had just dispersed had been identified by its chief, Matyana, as of local connection, though it might have been scouting for a larger force. If there were, in fact, a larger force, and that force intended to engage Chelmsford's centre column, then three propositions followed: firstly, the Zulu army had yet to reach the head of the plain in its march from Ulundi; secondly, it had already passed the head of the plain to north or south; thirdly, since only the north afforded an approach to Isandhlwana with any cover (the south approach involved crossing five miles of open plain), the corollary to proposition two was that the Zulu army was most likely above the camp on the Nqutu plateau.

Shortly before ten o'clock, while Chelmsford was stopped for breakfast above the Mangeni, a message reached him from Isandhlwana pointing very strongly to this conclusion. 'Report just come in,' ran a brief note delivered by mounted courier, 'that the Zulus are advancing in force from left front of the camp (i.e., across the plateau), 8.05 a.m.

At this juncture, doubtless happy to justify a role of some incongruity, a naval officer on the general staff climbed a tree and trained his telescope on the distant camp. It was too far away to make out much more than a white smudge of canvas against the darker spur, but he observed that things looked normal, though he thought the oxen had been moved closer to the troop lines. It seemed unlikely, therefore, that the reported advance had yet become an attack; indeed, there was no telling how long an assault, if it were intended, might be delayed. Had Chelmsford immediately assembled his troops and marched back to Isandhlwana, he could have been there by 1 pm, and sufficiently close by noon to have a psychological effect on the enemy. That he failed to do so has been explained by the view that the camp, even in its depleted condition, was well able to deal with any attack which might be mounted. Such a view, if contentious, was arguable. It is very difficult to find any argument in favour of Chelmsford's next step.

Before receiving Pulleine's word of the Zulu advance, the general had decided to situate a new camp in the Mangeni valley, below him as he rested, and a few miles nearer Ulundi than was Isandhlwana. He now despatched two officers, Major Stuart Smith, a gunner, and Captain Alan Gardner of staff transport, with orders that Pulleine should strike tents, forward them with baggage and provisions, then follow with his force to the Mangeni. Chelmsford also sent Browne and his battalion of levies to assist in the removal.

If the enemy was on the Nqutu in strength, poised above Isandhlwana, it would be hard to imagine a more imprudent operation than striking camp. Yet even at 12.30, when a spasm of artillery fire was heard from across the plain, and shells could be seen exploding on the Nqutu escarpment – a prisoner taken in the earlier skirmish was prompted to boast that Cetshwayo's army was attacking – Chelmsford showed no alarm, turning about when the firing stopped and descending to the Mangeni, preoccupied with plans for the new base. In the words of Captain Thomas Lucas of the Cape Rifles, 'not the faintest suspicion of any fatality seems to have crossed the minds of the general and his staff'.

Meanwhile, Browne, cursing and kicking his weary levies west across the hot plain, had been left far behind the mounted messengers, Smith and Gardner. Eight miles from Isandhlwana, he gave chase to, and captured, a Zulu youth who had been sent from the Nqutu to spy in the eastern hills. There were, blurted the boy, twelve Zulu regiments on the plateau, an army in the region of 20,000 warriors. Browne immediately scrawled a message to Chelmsford, thrust it into the hands of a European subordinate, and told him to ride back to the Mangeni post-haste.

A mile or so nearer the camp, Browne saw the flash of shell-bursts on the Nqutu and was able to distinguish the dark shape of Zulu formations atop the escarpment. Sending a second, and more urgent, note to Chelmsford, he urged his men forward. But the exhausted Kaffirs had seen enough of the situation to want no part of it. For all the blustering and bludgeoning of their NCOs, they refused to move more than a hundred yards, or thereabouts. Leaving them crouched in an inert mass, Browne rode forward alone to within four miles of Isandhlwana. There, a helpless speck on the baked veld, he watched the black wave of the Zulu impi pour over the edge of the plateau, swirl onto the plain and lap the entire camp. He did not wait to see more.

Spurring back to his cowed battalion, Browne retired it to the best defensible ground he could find, formed a ring with the officers in the centre, and prayed that Chelmsford would arrive in response to the earlier messages before it was too late. At that moment, Harness's gun battery was visible on the eastern heights, wending its way towards the Mangeni site. Once more, Browne despatched a messenger, this time with a desperate SOS.

Harness, who had followed the manoeuvring of Browne's levies with curiosity, unable to see beyond them to the distant camp, halted his column as the messenger galloped up. The note pushed into his hands astonished him. 'For God's sake come back with all your men,' it read, 'the camp is surrounded and must be taken unless helped.' A member of Chelmsford's staff, Major Matthew Gosset, was nearby, and Harness asked him to take the news to the general. Gosset, who seems to have regarded Browne's plea with scepticism, advised the artilleryman against diverting from his intended course, and rode off.

Arthur Harness was an old warrior, a plodder who might

never attain high distinction but who was sufficiently steeped in the family tradition of soldiering to respond intuitively to the distress signal of a fellow campaigner. The admonition of a 'staff wallah' did not overawe him. Wheeling his force, he set off at best speed towards Isandhlwana. He had not gone far before Gosset cantered back to him. The general's instructions were that the guns should proceed to the site of the new camp. Harness was stymied. He could not disregard a firm order.

Despite the sequence of messages from Pulleine, Browne and Harness, Chelmsford's preoccupation with establishing a new base on the Mangeni never faltered. Whatever his interpretation of the Isandhlwana action – and there is evidence that Gosset, attuned to the general's attitude, diluted the contents of Browne's final SOS – Chelmsford clearly failed to regard it as critical. Finally, at 2.45 that afternoon, with Glyn, Dartnell and Harness converging on the new camp, he decided to ride west with his staff and find out what all the fuss had been about. Soon after he set off, two messages direct from Isandhlwana bolstered his confidence. The first reported an action to the left of the camp; the second, that the Zulu in that region were 'falling back'.

When he reached the native battalion on the plain, and Browne confided grimly that Isandhlwana had fallen, Chelmsford was as incredulous as had been Browne to see the general approaching – not with his full force, but at the head of a small mounted escort. A low ridge concealed the camp from Browne's position. Chelmsford flatly discounted the astounding news. Browne was unreliable, a makeshift soldier. Ordering the battalion to fall in, the general nudged his horse and waved the frightened levies forward.

Chapter Five

ISANDHLWANA

*To the legion of the lost ones, to the
cohort of the damned*

Rudyard Kipling,
'Gentlemen Rankers'

I<small>N</small> compliance with Cetshwayo's command, the Zulu army
travelled slowly towards the invaders. It could have reached
Isandhlwana in two days – it took four. Indeed, on the first
night of its march, the 17th, it rested so close to Nodwengu, its
point of departure, that it might almost as well have stayed in
barracks and set out next morning. The old general Tshingwayo,
and his younger partner, Mavumengwana, appreciated the use-
fulness of a night in the field before advancing in earnest. It was
a long time since a full Zulu army had taken the war trail, and
the regiments needed to acclimatise to campaign discipline. The
initial lay-up, on the banks of the White Umfolosi, a few miles
west of Ulundi, enabled the indunas to sort out positions, and
their warriors to orientate themselves within the great host.

On the eighteenth, the impi left the Umfolosi, regiment after
black regiment falling into line of column, each with its dis-
tinctive shields, plumes and other honours: the uThulwana and
uDloko, comprising the Undi corps, the umKhulutshane and
Isangqu, comprising the Nodwengu corps, and the uNokenke,
uDududu, umCijo, umHlanga, uVe, inGobamakhosi, umBonambi

67

and inDlu-Yengwe. Few white men had seen such a sight. Fynn, the first Englishman to witness a march-past of Zulu regiments, had recorded the impressiveness of the scene – 'surprising to us, who could not have imagined that a nation termed "savages" could be so disciplined and kept in order'.

Cetshwayo did not accompany the army. Though he had done his military stint and, during Mpande's reign, won an internecine battle against a family rival, he was not a warrior-king and made no claim to generalship. Premier Mayamana travelled as a symbol of the state council, while the royal family was conspicuously represented by the king's brother, the bold Dabulamanzi, commander of the Undi contingent.

Many young Zulus of notable pedigree and tribal status marched not only as regimental captains but in the ranks, where their particular indignation at the British incursion added fire to the mood of their compatriots. Among them was Methlagazulu, a son of Sirayo, who served under Sigcwelegcwele in the inGobamakhosi. Outraged by Chelmsford's destruction of the family kraal, and the death of his kinsman, Methlagazulu anticipated battle with sombre relish.

The Zulu army looked to few ancillary services. Its medical facilities were restricted to the somewhat primitive physics carried by the inyangas, or healing doctors, whose standard treatment for wounds was a poultice of crushed leaves and a dose of boiled ox intestines, gall and herbs. Doubtless helped by the excellent fitness of the average Zulu warrior, recoveries were of a surprisingly high order. As a form of psychological therapy, wounded warriors were induced to spit on a stick, point it in the direction of the enemy and defy him with repeated shouts of *Yize!* (Come on!).

Few provisions were carried on active service. Teams of youths might follow the army with supplies of grain, but these were limited, and a force embarking on anything like a prolonged campaign relied on driven cattle or what it could plunder in enemy territory. Like all armies dependent to any extent on living off the land, the Zulu impi was at some disadvantage on home ground, where foraging presented problems in public relations. For this reason it camped, whenever feasible, in the region of established military kraals, which could generally scratch up a subsistence.

On the night of the 18th, Cetshwayo's army stopped at a barracks nine miles west of the Umfolosi; on the 19th, at a royal kraal about the same distance farther on. On the 20th, its march brought it to the vicinity of Isipezi, not far from the head of the plain across which lay the British camp, and here, for the first time, Tshingwayo and Mavumengwana ran into difficulties. Since there was no military kraal near Isipezi, the army spent the night in a shallow basin of land among the foothills, where it was situated the morning Dartnell and Lonsdale set out on their reconnaissance. For some reason now obscure, the local chief Matyana, whose kraal was just south of the Mangeni, here disputed the strategy of the Zulu generals. It seems probable that Matyana wanted the army deployed to oppose Dartnell and Lonsdale, each of whom, from his respective aspect, was working steadily towards the chief's lands. If this, in fact, were the dissident's proposal – and it is supported by Matyana's presence in the Zulu group which skirmished with the reconnaissance forces on the 22nd – it could only wreck the main chance of the impi, which lay in a surprise attack on the British camp.

At all events, Tshingwayo and Mavumengwana led their regiments north-west on the morning of the 21st, away from Matyana's lands, onto the Nqutu plateau, where they lay-up in a dry ravine about four miles short of the spur which sheltered the British tents. Matyana was no more trouble. During the skirmish in the eastern hills, where his followers were routed, he was personally pursued for three miles by a mounted British officer, narrowly escaping by plunging down a crevice.

The impi had done well. It was still fresh. It had advanced to within striking distance of the enemy without being spotted. It was comfortably hidden from sight of the vedettes on the escarpment, and beyond range of routine patrols from the British lines. So content was the Zulu command with the position that, having spent the night of the 21st uneventfully in the ravine, it was prepared to spend a further day and night there because the

moon was inauspicious for battle on the 2nd. There was just one
problem. The regiments had not had a proper meal since the
night of the 19th. They needed food. The indunas sent out their
foragers.

The foragers of the umCijo decided to search west, holding to
low ground to avoid the gaze of scouting enemies. There was
a number of small Zulu homesteads on the plateau, and on one
they found a few head of cattle. Driving the beasts before them,
the umCijo foragers headed back towards their regiment. It was
almost high sun, and they were mounting the slope which gave
on to the ravine, when a party of riders loomed on a ridge behind
them. The riders were black men, mounted on ponies. But they
wore uniforms and carried rifles. They were not Zulus.

Unarmed, their only succour the 20,000 strong impi concealed
in the ravine ahead, the umCijo herdsmen raced for the lip and
slid over. Already, the horsemen had started in hot pursuit.

ᏫᏋᏘᏐᏒ

Durnford and Pulleine had snatched a late breakfast that morning. The normal 7.30 breakfast parade at Isandhlwana had been
interrupted by reported Zulu movements on the plateau, and the
camp had been called to arms. It was thus that Durnford had
found things on his arrival from Rorke's Drift, though by then,
about 10 am, nothing had come of the reports, and tensions
had eased. Pulleine outlined the situation to the newcomer, detail-
ing his fighting strength as follows:

Five companies 1st/24th, one company 2nd/24th (this company
had been on outpost duty when the general had taken the rest
of the 2nd battalion), six companies NNC (four had been left
behind by Lonsdale, and two returned with captured cattle),
the best part of the Natal Mounted Police, and part of the artillery
battery. In approximate figures, this amounted to 600 imperial
infantry, 600 native foot, 100 cavalry and 70 artillerymen with
two pieces. The cavalry was occupied largely with vedette duties,
while a company of levies was posted on the neck of the spur

to prevent any infiltration of the crag immediately behind the camp.

From Rorke's Drift, Durnford had brought five troops of Natal Mounted Natives (recruited from horse-owning clans in the colony, well-trained and rifle-armed), altogether 250 men, three companies of foot levies, about 300 men, and a rocket battery. He had also brought a reserve of ammunition, increasing the camp's supply to half a million rounds. In addition to this strength, there was a considerable number of support personnel at Isandhlwana, both civilians employed on the transport and soldiers occupied in trades, orderly duties, medical work, and so on. The band of the 1st Battalion was detailed to provide stretcher-bearers in the event of an action; the drummer boys, some not yet in their teens, to act as ammunition-runners.

Pulleine was not a man for wasting words, but he appreciated the need to keep Chelmsford in touch with developments and had sent off the first of his messages at the time of the breakfast alert. On completing the belated meal, he despatched a subaltern to the vedettes on the Nqutu to obtain details of the latest situation there. The report was that the Zulus sighted earlier were retiring to the east along the plateau.

For the second time since the start of the invasion, Durnford now resolved on a personal initiative. The first had earned him a swift rebuke from the general; his new plan, aimed directly at supporting Chelmsford, could only redound, he seems to have supposed, to the credit of all involved. As Durnford saw it, Chelmsford was opposing the main Zulu force in the eastern hills. If the enemy on the plateau were retiring in that direction, the general's left flank was threatened from the rear. This could be obviated by a simple stratagem. The Zulu on the plateau should be followed and dispersed. A parallel advance should be made on the plain, beneath the escarpment, with a view to trapping them at the eastern end of the plateau.

To expedite this scheme, Durnford divided his mounted natives into two forces, sending one onto the Nqutu under Captain George Shepstone, while the other, together with the rocket battery, prepared to follow Durnford himself on the plain below.

Pulleine declined to contribute troops for the enterprise. If Durnford chose to deploy his own men in an independent adventure, that was his business. Pulleine was concerned only with the defence of the camp. He did, however, agree to send a company of British infantry, under Captain Charles Cavaye, to reinforce the company of the NNC on the spur. He was not entirely convinced of the position on the plateau. There might be more Zulus there than Durnford's men could manage.

Durnford quit camp between 11 am and mid-day, riding east with his cavalry at a pace which soon had the mule-borne rocket battery trailing. There was no sign of any Zulus on the plain, nor atop the escarpment to his left. At the same time, Shepstone, on the heights, was similarly drawing blank. Of the supposedly retiring enemy on the plateau, he saw none. After a while, he detached a troop of his riders in sections to comb the undulating ground to the north-west.

They were four miles from Isandhlwana when they caught their first glimpse of Zulu activity – an unprepossessing group of unarmed herdsmen driving a cluster of cattle. Without undue excitement, a section of cavalry started after them. Spurring up to a ridge over which the herdsmen had disappeared, the mounted troops came to an abrupt stop. Sprawled beneath them in the noon sun, a black mass swamping the slopes of the whole ravine, was an army of proportions beyond their wildest notions – regiment upon regiment of glistening, war-caparisoned warriors.

As the startled riders swung their ponies and raced back to warn the rest of their scattered troop, the Zulus began to swarm after them, like hornets from a disturbed nest. The discovered foragers had fled to their regimental position, and it was the umCijo, first alerted to the mounted scouts, who led the scramble from the ravine. Close behind, pounded the Nodwengu regiments. No induna needed the implications of discovery explained to him. It would be impossible to stop the horsemen transmitting their alarm to the British camp. Surprise now depended on pressing the assault without halt or hesitation. The tactics of the classic horned advance had been agreed for the morrow. Each regiment knew its place – and now knew that tomorrow would be too late.

Little more was required of Tshingwayo and Mavumengwana than their blessing. Shields hefted, assegais balanced, the warriors erupted from the ravine in a swelling mass. Only Dabulamanzi, with the Undi corps and the uDloko, were restrained by the generals, held back as the chest, or reserve, of the horned attack.

Shepstone's first warning was the bawling of his retreating scouts. Spurring to a vantage point, he was faced with the extraordinary sight of a mile-wide echelon of Zulus bearing down on him at a rhythmic lope. His first thought was for Durnford, on the plain below. Speeding messengers to alert him, Shepstone instructed a subordinate, Lieutenant Charles Raw, to impede the enemy as best possible with the mounted natives, and turned his own horse for Isandhlwana. A four-mile gallop brought him to the guard companies directly above the camp. Bellowing a warning, he slid his mount down the spur and burst into the tented lines. He found Pulleine reading Chelmsford's order, just arrived, to dismantle the camp and send the baggage on. Gasping for breath, Shepstone blurted the urgent news.

George Shepstone had seen a lot of Zulus, but by no means the whole of Cetshwayo's army. The impi had begun to separate into flanking and central units almost as soon as it had left the ravine, the uNokenke and uDududu forming the right horn, the umBonambi and inGobamakhosi forming the left, with the rest of the regiments fanning out as they advanced to fill some two or more miles in between. Pulleine therefore received a dramatic warning, but not a comprehensive one. He now joined the chain of British officers, from Dartnell and Lonsdale to Chelmsford himself, and on to Durnford, who had based portentous decisions on a grave underestimation of the enemy.

Weakened though Isandhlwana had been by Chelmsford's departure, it still counted (including Durnford's strength) 600 imperial infantry, 350 cavalry, 900 foot levies, two field guns and a rocket battery – apart from casuals. With considerably fewer men, Andries Pretorius had smashed a Zulu army without losing a single Boer. Moreover, Pretorius, whose fighters were not professionals, had had to rely on muskets, not rifles. He had done it in part by fighting from laager, in part by an astute choice of ground, but fundamentally by concentrating his firepower in a compact mass and inviting the enemy to destroy himself in a hail of withering volley fire.

Pulleine had no time, at this moment, to haul his wagons into the defensive wall Chelmsford had neglected, but he would have had time to congregate his troops in tight defensive formation, backed by the protecting spur, and to muster his noncombatants in their midst. Instead, seemingly in the belief that the Zulus could be halted above the spur, he sent another company of the 1st/24th, under Captain William Mostyn, to join Cavaye's company and the levies on the heights. The remaining four infantry companies were now stretched very thinly ahead of the camp on a wide front, the artillery on a knoll left of centre facing the escarpment. The residue of the NNC was clustered a few hundred yards behind the sketchy red line of the 24th, between it and the tents, while the mounted contingent in camp took position by the wagons on the humped pass.

It was a disposition adequate perhaps to repelling an attack by the sort of moderately-sized and irresolute native force not infrequently encountered by the British in their empire exploits. Yet if two facts had been stressed incessantly – by sources as disparate as the Boers, the British settlers, the missionaries, the Natal natives, even Sir Bartle Frere himself – they were that the Zulu army was neither modest in size nor irresolute.

On the plateau, Raw and his troop could make no impression on the surging horde. Shooting from pony-back was inaccurate, and dismounting was dangerous. The fleet Zulus advanced with disconcerting rapidity. When the sound of firing above the camp suddenly intensified, Pulleine and his men knew that the companies guarding the spur were in action. Word had already been sent back to Chelmsford that a removal of camp was impossible at present. Now, a second messenger was despatched to report the heavy firing on the plateau. A qualifying missive to the effect that the enemy was falling back – the last Chelmsford received before joining Browne – appears to have had no basis save sheer

Battle of Isandhlwana   22 Jan. 1879

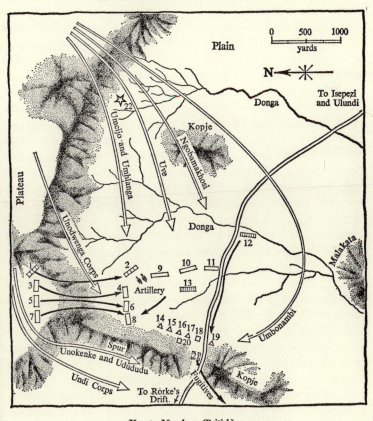

Key to Numbers (British)

1.	N.N.C. at start	12.	Durnford's Mounted
2.	N.N.C. later	13.	N.N.C. main body
3.	Cavaye at start	14.	N.N.C. camp lines
4.	Cavaye later	15.	N.N.C. camp lines
5.	Mostyn at start	16.	2nd - 24th
6.	Mostyn later	17.	R.A.
7.	Dyson	18.	Mounted contingent
8.	Younghusband	19.	1st - 24th
9.	Porteus	20.	H.Q.
10.	Wardell	21.	Wagons
11.	Pope	22.	Rocket Battery destroyed

wishful thinking. As the two couriers nudged their mounts briskly away from the alerted camp, there was still nothing to indicate the full measure of their good luck.

It was not until the levies on the spur came streaming down into camp, followed in more orderly retreat by the companies of Cavaye and Mostyn, then Raw and his mounted troops, that some idea of the weight of the enemy became evident to Pulleine. Since this was manifest, so far, only on the left flank, he withdrew a further company of the 1st/24th, under Captain Reginald Younghusband, from the front of camp and sent it to strengthen Cavaye and Mostyn, who had turned about on the plain at the base of the spur and formed line facing north to the escarpment. This allowed a mere three companies of imperial infantry – two from the 1st battalion under a Captain Wardell and a Lieutenant Porteous, and the single company from the 2nd battalion under Lieutenant Charles D'Aguilar Pope – to cover nearly a thousand yards of front – one man for about every three yards. True, they had the levies behind them, but these had already proved of poor mettle when hard-pressed.

Durnford was more than two miles out from the camp, riding close beneath the plateau, when one of Shepstone's messengers bore down on him, riding furiously. Almost simultaneously, Durnford sighted the reason for the man's haste. The entire skyline of the escarpment from his near left back to the spur itself had suddenly bristled with warriors. As he watched, momentarily mesmerised, their ranks thickened, poised on the rim for a brief spell, then poured over and deluged the near plain. He was directly in the path of the left horn. Wheeling his cavalry, he commenced an abrupt retreat, increasingly forced to his left by the Zulus swarming off the plateau. By interspersing his flight with judicious bursts of rifle fire, Durnford at last reached the cover of a donga to the right front of the camp, a short way ahead of Pope's company, where the horsemen dismounted and took a defensive stand.

Trailing far to Durnford's rear, the rocket battery, with its laden mules, had not stood a remote chance. The officer in charge had managed to unleash a couple of missiles as the Zulus blackened the escarpment, then he and his men were swamped in a human wave. Remarkably, three of them, left for dead by the onrushing warriors, survived their wounds to recount their tale later.

Few were so lucky. The army intelligence report on what followed was compiled, of grim necessity, very largely on the word of non-British, or unreliable irregular witnesses, and the graphic but all too silent evidence afterwards found on the battle site. Much of Isandhlwana remains, in consequence, a ghost battle illuminated by fragmentary and macabre testimony – a grisly visitation, as it proved, upon Victorian society, which quickly dismissed it to the darkest corner of its military graveyard.

By 12.30, when Chelmsford and his staff heard the distant gunfire, the entire British line was in action. At first, according to the intelligence document, the pressure was greatest on the left, where the regiments from Nodwengu were gushing from the spur against Mostyn, Cavaye and Younghusband, and on the contiguous elbow of the defence, where the umCijo and um-Hlanga threatened the artillery and a forward company of NNC. The gunners, having bombarded the escarpment with explosive, prepared to load case as the Zulus pressed in across the flat ground. The left horn of the impi, with farther to travel across the plain, and stung by fire from Durnford's retreating cavalry, took longer to mass against the British right. Ominously, a stream of umBonambi was curling to the far south, bent on outflanking the defensive line across the camp front and linking with the extremity of the right horn, already working round the back of the spur towards the rear of the humped pass.

Still, at this stage, the defenders were not dismayed. With some equanimity, the professional redcoat could survey a target so dense it hardly admitted a wasted shot. Dozens of the enemy were dropping with each British volley, sending ripples of hesitation through the masses around them, littering the plain with dead and dying. 'The places of the Zulus who fell were constantly filled by comrades', recorded a witness in the *Daily News*, but there was a limit to reckless bravery, and, as the range closed to three or four hundred yards, the severity of the punishment drove the leading warriors to fling themselves prone in the coarse grass. Shocked and frustrated, the Zulu wave subsided.

It was the classic situation Pulleine and his officers expected. The enemy, his own limited firearms ineptly handled, appeared to have shot his bolt. To the right front, Durnford was pacing the edge of the donga, scornfully exposed to the Zulus, encouraging his men to pepper the crouched and murmuring inGobamakhosi. The loose left sleeve of his jacket dangled heroically. Nobody, now, could mistake him for a mere road-mender in uniform. On the left flank, Cavaye and his compatriots of the 1st battalion had the umKhulutshane and the Isangqu pinned down at the perfect killing range. At the elbow of the British line, a gun crew aligned its field piece on a cluster of warriors sheltering behind a frail hut. The shell scored a direct hit.

In the Zulu ranks, dual calls of discipline and destiny struggled with the stunning effect of volley fire. No such impasse had been predicted. When Cetshwayo had instructed his army to advance slowly, he had not meant that it should cringe and crawl in the face of the enemy. The Zulu army was not a national minority which could vent its humiliation on absent countrymen; it was no less than the nation in arms – and that nation was being scorned by the redcoat invaders. Frustration gave way to mounting anger. Especially in the young and eager inGobamakhosi, stung by some of the heaviest casualties, warriors such as Methlagazulu boiled to get to grips with the lethal British riflemen.

Their chance came in the region of one o'clock – about the time Chelmsford's battalions could have been back at Isandhlwana had he acted on Pulleine's first report of a Zulu advance in force. Indeed, had the general then marched to reinforce the camp, his column must have been seen when the Zulus topped the escarpment, and their plans aborted, or significantly modified.

As it was, the rapacity of the defensive fire had depleted the pouches of the marksmen as swiftly as it had culled the enemy, and with considerably more speed than the quartermasters were dispensing ammunition. Runners from the lines, some with more than a mile to trundle to the reserve wagons, were arriving in hot, breathless groups, not always at the stores assigned to their battalions. Amidst the clamour, the quartermasters worked lugubriously, retarded by the heavily nailed and banded ammo-boxes and their own dour adherence to regulations. Though stocks were plentiful, runners arriving at the wrong wagons were sent away empty-handed. Those from native units, with little or no understanding of English, were bemused.

When line officers, patience exhausted, came to check on the delay, tempers ran high. In some instances, bayonets and rifle-butts were used to tackle the stubborn crates. Meanwhile, their troops were obliged to reduce fire.

It was what the Zulus had been waiting for. Rid of the devastating storm of lead, the inGobamakhosi clambered to their feet, followed by the uVe and the umCijo. One after another, the regiments rose, bellowing their scorn, stamping their feet, thumping their shields with their assegais. With a great roar of 'uSuthu!' – the name coined for Cetshwayo's partisans in his early days – the Zulu host surged forward. 'They came on,' one report had it, 'in regular battalions, eight deep,' this time undismayed by the fresh fire which raked them. It was too much for the levies at the elbow of the British line. Discarding their weapons, they fled back through the camp, along with most of their European NCOs, and disappeared through the humped pass. With them went the NNC reserves behind the front companies of the 24th.

In the next few moments, the battle passed irredeemably beyond British hands. Once its barrier of fire was broken, the over-extended line of outnumbered redcoats had no chance – scarcely time to fix bayonets. With the umCijo and umHlanga pouring through the gap left by the levies, the British wings made a belated attempt to withdraw towards the solid backing of the spur. On the right, D'Aguilar Pope, grasping a revolver and wearing his monocle, watched Durnford's cavalry pound back down the track towards the wagons, and knew that his flank was open. Ordering his bugler to sound 'Retire', he began to inch his company after Durnford. On the far left, Younghusband was trying to organise his own men into a defensive group while retreating to the stone wall behind the camp.

Elsewhere, there was chaos as the Zulus swept through and

behind the lines. Mostyn, Cavaye, Wardell and Porteous were engulfed where they stood, their isolated redcoats struggling hopelessly against the odds, like exotic insects overrun by black ants. Amid the tents and wagons, individuals and small groups of defenders fought with the rage of desperation in the swirling mass. Zulu warriors described later how parties of British soldiers held them off at bayonet point, cursing and taunting them, and how the Zulus hurled corpses on the blades before rushing in to kill their enemies.

Fragmentary glimpses of the last frenetic moments of human life have survived as agonising portions of a grotesque and incomplete jigsaw. A corporal of the 24th was believed to have spitted four warriors with his bayonet before being overwhelmed. A sailor, brought along as a servant with Chelmsford's staff, was seen holding off a swarm of Zulus with a cutlass, his back to a wagon wheel. Eventually, he was stabbed from behind, between the spokes. A Natal settler with the volunteer forces was found dead with his back to a boulder near the medical tent, where he had been under treatment. Almost a hundred spent cartridges lay on the ground with his empty revolver. A blood-encrusted bowie-knife was still in his hand. A drummer boy was discovered hanging from a wagon, his throat slit.

Younghusband had managed to rally about sixty of his company on a low ledge of the spur, where they fought shoulder to shoulder until swept away by sheer numbers. Grasping a rifle and bayonet, Younghusband dodged from wagon to wagon, lunging at all who came near, until he was shot by a Zulu with a British carbine.

Pope, with the remnants of the right wing, fought his way to the humped pass. Here, he found Durnford, with George Shepstone and about seventy of the mounted men. Theirs was the most significant stand, for Durnford, hoarse from bellowing orders above the din, had made a constructive attempt to secure a line of retreat to the west. While their ammunition lasted, the men in the pass held the tips of the Zulu horns apart with a telling volley fire before falling, last rounds spent, to the assegais.

Among the Zulus attacking Durnford was Methlagazulu. His

regiment had paid expensively since dropping from the plateau to the plain.

> We were fired on first by the mounted men [he recalled later] who checked our advance for some time. About now, our other regiments became engaged with soldiers who were in skirmishing order. When we pressed on, the mounted men retired to the donga, where they stopped us twice. We lost heavily from their fire. My regiment [the inGobamakhosi] suffered most. When we saw we could not drive them out of the donga, we extended our horn to the bottom of it, the lower part crossing and advancing on the camp in a semi-circle. When the mounted men saw this, they came out of the donga and galloped to the camp. Our horn suffered greatly, not only from the mounted troops but in crossfire from the white soldiers.
>
> As we advanced, the Nodwengu regiments of the right horn circled the sill [spur] to stop the road, the main body closing on the camp. I then heard a bugle call and saw some soldiers massing together. The soldiers had fired at a terrible rate, but suddenly stopped, and some began running.
>
> We didn't take any notice of those running away, thinking the end of our horn would catch them, but went for those who remained. They got into and under wagons, but we killed all of them there. Next, we came on a mixed party of mounted and foot who must have been stopped by the points of the horns beyond the pass. They numbered about a hundred. They resisted desperately, some firing, some using swords. I repeatedly heard the command 'Fire!' shouted; but we proved too many for them, and killed them all where they stood. When it was over, I had a look at these men and saw an officer with his arm in a sling, and with a big moustache, surrounded by carbineers and men I could not identify.

For most, the concept of retreat had been illusory. The first to test it, the fleeing Kaffirs, had quickly found the track to Rorke's Drift thick with waiting Zulus. Veering left down a steeply-banked watercourse, the majority attempted to make their way south-west to the Buffalo. Cetshwayo's men mopped them up avidly. The camp artillery officers, committed to saving their guns, had tried the same escape line. Whipping their trace horses into a mad dash, they had careered through the pass, hurtled headlong into the Zulu gauntlet, lost control of the heavy gun carriages and ended in a tangled mass on the banks of the watercourse. The Zulus later recovered the guns and dragged them to Ulundi.

Few Europeans, none of them dismounted men, reached the Buffalo, four miles distant. Of the handful of riders who did, most were drowned attempting to cross, or killed on the river banks. So inconsiderable was the number of exhausted and terror-haunted survivors who eventually reached safety in Natal, that it was widely held, even there, that the slaughter had been complete. 'You will have seen of our great disaster at Isandhlwana, only a short distance from the border,' ran a letter from Durban published in the *Daily News*, 'where every man was butchered ... it is evident that our general was out-generalled by the Zulus.'

Of some 1,800 men at Isandhlwana at the start of the action – more than half Europeans – perhaps 350 at last found a way to safety, the overwhelming majority of them Kaffirs. The six companies of the 24th Foot Regiment, comprising 21 officers and 581 other ranks, died to a man.

Pulleine had watched the débâcle from a vantage point behind the British centre front. When all was clearly lost, he hastened to the guard tent of the 1st battalion of the 24th, thrust the battalion colours into the hands of his adjutant, Teignmouth Melville, and charged him with securing them from the enemy. Pulleine was stabbed to death in the tent shortly afterwards, as Melville, spurred pell-mell along the Zulu-infested path to the Buffalo.

It was a hair-raising ride in which he can have had little time to contemplate the bodies already strewn there, or the anguished efforts of fellow fugitives to elude the pouncing spearmen. Somewhere near him rode Lieutenant Nevill Coghill of the High Commissioner's staff, whose horse streamed blood from an assegai wound in the quarters, and a Private Williams, groom to Glyn, who had been left in camp to mind the colonel's reserve mounts. The best of these Williams had picked for his escape bid. He was lucky. The animal eventually bore him to safety while lesser beasts fell exhausted by the gallop.

Melville's horse was so blown by the time he reached the river that it sank beneath the swift stream. Still clutching the colours, Melville struggled to stay afloat. Zulu shot was spattering around him. Coghill, who had somehow reached the far bank mounted, now turned bravely to the rescue. His horse had barely re-entered the river when it was shot dead. Unbeaten, Coghill struck out for Melville and hauled him to dry land. By now, the colours had succumbed to the torrent. Swept from Melville's grasp, they fetched up at the bottom of a still pool where, remarkably, they were recovered by the British at a later date. The two men got little farther. The Zulus were in wait for them.

'Not many yards from the riverside,' wrote the officer who found their bodies, 'are two boulders near the rocky path. At these boulders they made their last stand, and fought until over-whelmed. We found them lying side by side.' Melville's watch had stopped at 2.10 pm.

Chapter Six

RORKE'S
DRIFT

Ni ngama qawu!
You are heroes!
Zulu salutation.

As Melvill, Coghill and the other fugitives careered south-west in their frantic dash, a lone rider wended slowly towards the camp across the plain from the south-east. The fat Lonsdale and his diminutive pony, Dot, were a combination of some fun to the British troops with Chelmsford, but neither of the pair was amused at that moment. The long-suffering animal had carried her overweight cargo too far, on too little food, since leaving Isandhlwana at dawn on the 21st, to go much further. Lonsdale, groggy from his recent concussion, incipient fever and lack of sleep, had only one thought: to get his head down for an hour or so.

With this priority, and the secondary objective of supervising the removal of the NNC headquarters to the new site, he had descended alone to the plain after the morning's skirmish in the eastern hills and pointed Dot's hungry nose towards the distant tents. She had needed no directing. Reins relaxed, Lonsdale drowsed spasmodically in a sticky saddle.

Approaching the camp lines, he was jerked upright by a report and the whistle of a bullet. Lonsdale mistook the warrior who had fired it for one of his own levies. Their trigger-happy propensities were not strange to him, and a bustle of red tunics in the background impressed his cloudy mind with normality. He was within a few yards of the nearest tents, and preparing to dismount, when a chill revelation bore in on him. The men in red had black faces and carried assegais. The blades of the assegais dripped blood.

For a moment, Lonsdale gawped about him, horrified. Everywhere he looked, Zulu warriors, many wearing tunics and sun helmets stripped from their enemies, were ransacking the camp, looting tents, breaking open crates of ammunition. Incredibly, their preoccupation with plunder had so far secured his survival. Yanking wildly at Dot's head, he reversed course and whipped up a feeble trot. The ghastliness of the scene was mounting in his giddy head. Bodies festooned the camp site, imbrued in their own gore, many slashed open and disembowelled in accord with the Zulu custom of releasing the 'evil spirits' of their dead foes.

With terrifying gradualness, the pony stumbled from the battleground and heaved her belabouring load east. Less than a mile from the lines, she gave up. Sliding from the saddle, Lonsdale looked back. Miraculously, there was no pursuit. Leading the exhausted animal, he continued his solitary retreat on foot. He was near prostration himself when he saw Browne's battalion approaching, headed by Chelmsford and his escort. The encounter probably saved the general a further disaster, for there were still thousands of Zulu in the camp towards which he was advancing with cool self-assurance. Confronted by Lonsdale, he could no longer doubt the presence of calamity.

Sending urgent word to Glyn to return with his entire force immediately, Chelmsford settled grimly to wait three miles short of Isandhlwana. The camp had fallen, but Lonsdale could not tell the extent of the losses. It seemed reasonable to suppose that some portion of the garrison had withdrawn towards Rorke's Drift.

Glyn received the general's message at 4 pm and rapidly formed column at the site of the new camp. His men had been marching, with little rest, since daylight, but the sense of crisis revitalised weary limbs and they tackled the long tramp westward doggedly.

They reached Chelmsford at 6.10, almost too tired to take in the preposterous tidings. A bemused cheer greeted the general's announcement that they would immediately advance and retake the camp. With the mounted men ahead, the six companies of 2nd/24th in extended line, guns in the centre, the column lurched forward.

Daylight was waning. To the front, smoke from burning tents smudged a lowering sky. To the right, the darkening silhouette of the Nqutu was stippled with retiring Zulus.

It was almost dark when the troops blundered on the first cold bodies, and halted. From here, a short barrage of shrapnel shell was dropped on the humped pass before the guns were advanced to open fire again. Since no response was encountered, three companies of infantry were sent in to probe the shattered and twilit camp. It was devoid of life, save for a few Zulus intoxicated from the plundered stores. These besotted stragglers were promptly despatched at bayonet point. Dusk concealed the worst of the ravages as the main force groped forward amid nightmare shadows to bivouac in the wagon park.

Few slept that night. Somewhere on the plateau, a drunken Zulu periodically discharged a firearm. Elsewhere, a dying warrior groaned in the darkness. Terrified Kaffirs, their faith in British arms shattered, dissolved from their battalions in shady groups, and only a guard of infantry constrained a mass exodus. Chelmsford, tall and gaunt, paced the lines like a brooding wraith. All faced the new day with foreboding.

Dawn exceeded their worst fears. Apart from the count of dead comrades, more than a hundred wagons were destroyed, 1,400 oxen slaughtered or driven off, two seven-pounder guns captured with 400 rounds of shell, 800 rifles with 250,000 rounds of ammunition lost, and commissariat supplies looted or ruined to the value of £60,000. Not only was the central column smashed and the plan of campaign wrecked – the very survival of the force remaining with Chelmsford was precarious.

Had Chelmsford been attacked in strength that night, his men must have shared the fate of those stretched around them. His force was low in spirit, energy and ammunition, and targets would have been hard to spot in the black shadows of Isandhlwana. Indeed, on home ground, with his numerical superiority, natural agility and silence of movement, the Zulu had much to gain from nocturnal action. It would, however, have meant innovation, and the warrior mentality was ever oddly inflexible. Just as the British army, in the age of the rifle, still advertised its whereabouts in red serge (the most conspicuous target colour in the spectrum), so the African soldier clung to his faith in war display and regalia – the idea that his potency was closely linked with visual impact. The Zulus were not accustomed to fighting in darkness, and Cetshwayo had expressly forbidden the experiment.

Nor, for that matter, were African armies accustomed to fighting pitched battles in quick succession. Tactically and logistically, they were geared to the decisive set-piece, the emphasis on the build-up rather than the aftermath. Like the armies of early medieval Europe, the Zulu host expected to retire and lick its wounds at some leisure after battle, especially since the shock of a costly affray, even a victorious one, could reverberate grievously through a small nation. At Isandhlwana, Cetshwayo's regiments had paid for their extraordinary persistence with at least 2,000 dead and as many more badly wounded – a tenth of the country's manhood stricken in a single day. The regiments which finally withdrew from the holocaust wanted only to disperse to their kraals and recuperate.

One part alone of the impi which marched on Isandhlwana remained relatively unscarred – the Undi corps and the uDloko regiment, which, under Dabulamanzi, had been held in reserve on the plateau at the time of the horned attack. With the assault in full swing, Tshingwayo had assigned Dabulamanzi the task of cutting the British line of retreat, at the same time preventing any possible enemy reinforcement from Natal by way of Rorke's Drift.

Swinging wide round the top of the spur, the swaggering captain of the royal house had led his contingent, 4,000 strong, west across the Nqutu, outside the right horn of the main force, and dropped down on to the track half a mile or more in the rear of the humped pass. Here, he had sat his men down to await developments. Alongside the uDloko, a married regiment, was the uThulwana, also married, and the bachelor inDlu-Yengwe. Of these formations, only the last was to see action in the ensuing engagement, and that was not in a very exacting role. The inDlu-Yengwe had been detached to mop up the fugitives heading for the Buffalo. With the horns of the main army circling the spur, and resistance in the British camp fizzling to cessation, Dabulamanzi had soon become restless.

Rousing the two head-ringed regiments, he had marched southwest, crossed the river and settled on the far bank until the inDlu-Yengwe rejoined him, its mopping-up mission accomplished. The entire force now moved upstream, Dabulamanzi leading on a white horse, the uThulwana with white shields and ostrich plumes in their head-dresses, the uDloko with red shields daubed with white spots, the inDlu-Yengwe with black shields, white-spotted, and thick cowtail necklaces. They were treading the Natal bank, and Cetshwayo had proscribed an invasion of the colony, but it was a fine point, and Dabulamanzi was in no mood to split hairs.

Four miles ahead, he could re-cross the river at Rorke's Drift. At Rorke's Drift there should be some British soldiers. He had no desire to return to barracks with the only regiments in the army whose spears were unbloodied.

The sequestered crossing at Rorke's Drift was overlooked by a bleak, rocky outcrop, the Oskarberg, on the Natal bank, tucked under the western terrace of which stood a Swedish mission station comprising two single-storey stone buildings with thatched roofs. Close by was the initial invasion camp of the centre column, now deserted save for a single company of the 2nd/24th, about eighty bayonets, and a small party of levies.

The mission house had been requisitioned by the army as a hospital; the second building as a store, now packed with mealie sacks and biscuit boxes. Otto Witt, the resident missionary, an excitable man whose relationships were poor on both sides of the border, had sent his family off to Pietermaritzburg and was living, obligingly, in a tent.

The gunfire at Isandhlwana had registered with interest, but no great urgency, at Rorke's Drift. The general, it was known, had gone looking for the Zulu army, and the officers at the outpost assumed that he had found at least part of it. Over lunch, Major Henry Spalding, in charge of the column's line of communications, decided to ride west to Helpmakaar, the nearest army station in Natal, and fetch up one of two infantry companies posted there. He set off on the ten-mile journey at 2 o'clock, leaving the personnel at the drift to their routine tasks of nursing the sick, cleaning equipment, tending the pontoons and filling holes in the wagon track. There were now three regular officers at the post, of whom Surgeon Major James Reynolds, a thirty-five-year-old Irishman, was concerned solely with medical duties.

If it occurred to his companions that life was less than exciting in the middle of nowhere, they were not unaccustomed to being overlooked. At thirty-two, Lieutenant John Chard, Royal Engineers, who commanded precisely one enlisted sapper at Rorke's Drift, had been looking forward to promotion for thirteen years. Thickly-bearded, with large bones and an impressively bridged nose, he might have passed, in other garb, as a Jewish patriarch. He remained, for all that, a long-standing junior.

Still, Chard clung to hopes which appeared to have deserted Gonville Bromhead, a year older and holding the same rank. Bromhead, commanding the company of 24th at the outpost, was rich in attributes which might have been expected to secure his advancement. A son of Sir Edmond de Gonville Bromhead of Thurlby Hall, Lincolnshire, whose family traditionally sent its scions to the 24th Foot, 'Gonny' Bromhead's social assets included not only darkly handsome features, with intense eyes and a trim, debonair moustache, but more importantly a brother of senior rank in the regiment. He had, however, an overriding disadvantage. Prematurely encroaching deafness had reduced his hearing to a critically low ebb. Uncertain of comprehending verbal orders, or even normal conversation, he was moody and unpopular with many men. His superiors looked to his future with grave doubts.

At about three o'clock in the afternoon, Chard was inspecting the pontoons on the river when he heard shouting and saw horsemen galloping from Isandhlwana. Putting their foam-flecked mounts through the water, they reined-in beside him and blurted the news that the camp had been overpowered by the Zulu army, a strong section of which was now marching towards Rorke's Drift. The two riders were NNC subalterns. Having abandoned Isandhlwana at the time the levies fled, they had somehow eluded the Zulu guard on the main track. One now prepared to ride on with the tidings to Helpmakaar, while the other, a Lieutenant James Adendorff, promised to stay and help Chard and Bromhead. In fact, though some secondary sources list Adendorff at the defence of the outpost, no primary account of the action mentions him, and several witnesses reported that he rode off beforehand.

Chard retraced the quarter-mile from the pontoons to the mission station in bewilderment. An attack on the drift had, of course, always been a possibility since the column left on the 20th, but no one had contemplated more than a raiding party. The place was simply not prepared against any form of mass assault.

With Bromhead, he reviewed the situation. The first thoughts of both men were retreat, and there was some talk of it, though the reported proximity of the Zulus made the notion a wishful one. It was finally quashed by the acting commissariat officer, a sergeant-major of long service named James Dalton, who bluntly proclaimed it suicidal. Thirty-five sick men in the hospital – a few wounded in the early action against Sirayo's kraal, more feverish – could not be made ready, and wagons spanned and loaded, in under sixty minutes at the very least. If the Zulus had

Defences at Mission Station, Rorkes Drift

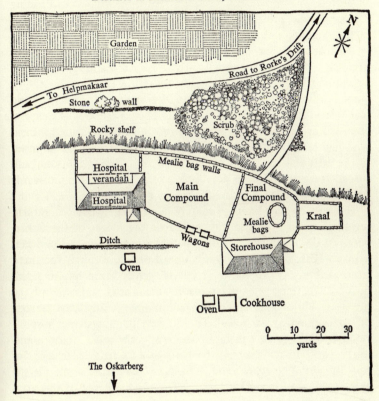

not arrived in that time, they would rapidly overhaul the retiring force.

Poor as the prospects appeared, it had to be better to stand
at the mission, and hope that Spalding returned with help before
it was overrun. The odds improved somewhat when a troop of
perhaps a hundred mounted natives, under a European officer,
suddenly rode up. They had been escorting Durnford's delayed
wagon train to Isandhlwana when the camp was attacked, and
had turned back at the last moment. They were well-armed and
regarded as steady men – a reputation justified by their brothers
who had fallen with Durnford. Despatching this force as vedettes
to the drift and the flanks of the Oskarberg, Chard and Bromhead
turned their attention to defensive works. At the moment, apart
from the two thatched buildings, none existed.

The mission faced approximately north-west. Behind it, screening the approach of Dabulamanzi, rose the ledges of the Oskarberg. To the front was flat land patchily covered with low bush,
across which, some thirty yards ahead of the hospital, the track
from Helpmakaar to the drift curved gently from left to right.
Beyond the track was the mission garden and, a few yards to
the near side of it, a stone wall about sixty yards long, trailing
off to nothing at each end. Of the two buildings, the hospital
stood to the left as one faced the track; the store house about
thirty yards to its right, set back so that its front corresponded
roughly with the rear of the hospital. Apart from a small rectangular kraal of stone hard-by the front-right corner of the store
house, there was nothing near the buildings to constitute a
barrier.

Unlike their superiors at Isandhlwana, the subalterns at the
mission were in no doubt about the need to fight within a pro-
tective wall. The tented camp offered no defence at all, and
the tents were struck. With the only building materials swiftly
available – the stockpiled biscuit boxes and mealie bags – Chard
and Bromhead made the best of the works already standing.

From the left-front corner of the hospital, extending forward
about ten yards, then sweeping clear across the front of both
buildings to join with the front wall of the kraal, they planned

a barricade of boxes and mealie sacks, roughly chest high. With the rear-left of the kraal similarly linked to the nearby front-right of the store house, it would remain to barricade between the front-left of the store house and the right-rear of the hospital to provide a complete, if rather straggling, perimeter. When loop-holes were knocked in the walls of the two buildings, any aspect of the enclosure could be covered by fire from behind some protection. It was primitive, but, as the men slowly built up the sections, they began to glimpse at least an impression of safety. To fill up the rear wall more rapidly, two wagons were incorporated in its length.

By 4.30, the greater part of the wall was assembled, and a human chain was toiling to raise the last section – that immediately to the front of the hospital – when a cry was heard from a look-out on the Oskarberg. He had just sighted the regiments through glasses. They were, he yelled, 'black as hell and thick as grass'.

Suddenly, danger clinched beyond question, the mood changed. As the small band of redcoats ceased labouring, snatched rifles and fixed bayonets, a lesson in human nature proceeded which disheartened and angered them. First, a single horseman pulled on to the track and disappeared towards Helpmakaar at a gallop. It was the missionary Witt getting out while there was still time. Next, the mounted natives appeared, riding pell-mell from the vedette posts. Without pausing even to glance at the mission station, they fled after Witt, towards safety, their officer pausing long enough to apologise. His men, he said, were terror-stricken; they refused to obey him. He then galloped after them.

Finally, the Kaffirs stationed at the outpost rushed to the barricades, scrambled over and raced off behind the mounted troops, accompanied by their European NCOs and their officer, a Captain Stephenson. The sight was too much for some of the British soldiers. Angry shouts went up from the ranks, a shot was heard, and one of the fleeing NNC sergeants fell with a bullet in him.

Chard turned his bushy face to the reserve of boxes and sacks still piled in front of the store house. It was no time to be quibbling over the shooting of a deserter. The total of men in the post was now reduced to 139, of whom 35 were hospital cases. Clearly, this was too small a force to man the whole of the improvised perimeter effectively. A further barrier of biscuit boxes was therefore hastily extended from the left wall of the store house forward to the front of the perimeter, thus forming a smaller enclosure with two substantial sides – the kraal and the store house – within the larger one. While this compound at the eastern end of the enclave would be more easily defensible than the whole, its occupation raised a fresh problem. Before the original defences could be drawn in, the hospital at the western end would have to be evacuated and the patients shifted some fifty yards between the buildings.

There was scarcely time to consider it. A general shout of warning went up as the vanguard of Dabulamanzi's regiments suddenly loped into sight round the Oskarberg. The leading force was the bachelor inDlu-Yengwe, some six hundred of whom advanced on the rear of the mission at a brisk trot while the remainder of their comrades, with the uThulwana and uDloko, swept round the west of the outpost, past the left wall of the hospital, towards the front. The first defensive shots burst from the loopholes in the back of the hospital, and from behind the rear barricade of wagons and mealie bags, as the inDlu-Yengwe raced to within a score of yards from the south wall and dived for cover behind some ovens and a small stone cookhouse.

There was little other shelter at the back, and, frustrated by the fire from the blank walls of the hospital, the bulk of the initial assault party swirled left to follow the main Zulu deployment round the building, or recoiled to the lower ledges of the Oskarberg, where those with firearms began to snipe into the enclave. Their marksmanship, for the most part wild and ineffective, contrasted starkly with the British shooting. One rifleman on the rear wall, a Private Dunbar, killed eight Zulus with eight successive shots.

Meanwhile, streaming to the west front, the leading wave of warriors broke on the incomplete barrier of sacks and boxes in a howling torrent. Ignoring their losses, the Zulu spearmen clambered on to the barricades, and it seemed that the post must be deluged. In these opening moments of the action, the viability of the defence received its sternest test. Shoulder to shoulder, firing and reloading with frenetic industry, lunging with bayonet at those who came closest, Bromhead's men held their line intact. The Zulus, halted, piled up in a dense mass. Obstructed by the sheer weight of flesh, dead and crippled, fronting the barricade, perhaps thoughtful that the small band of defenders might be vanquished less expensively with a little more patience, the warriors in the rear ranks stopped pressing. Its impetus expended, the early charge subsided.

Two precautions were already proving their worth to the British force: firstly, the front barricade had been sited on a slight ridge which increased the height of its outer face to the extent that the enemy, for all his agility, was unable to vault it, but had to use his hands and arms to scramble over. This gave the defenders an advantage, both in height and the free use of weapons; secondly, the defenders had had the foresight to break open a large number of ammunition boxes prior to the engagement, and rounds were liberally available.

Nevertheless, the situation was desperate. To the front, the bush, the track and the garden beyond swarmed with several thousand Zulus, and Dabulamanzi, directing operations from a clump of trees thirty yards or so ahead of the hospital, was soon throwing in fresh attacks. They came, billow upon bristling billow, roaring 'uSuthu!', leaping the mounds of their own dead, to hurl themselves at the slashed and reddening mealie bags.

Bromhead had grabbed a rifle and darted behind the line of defenders, screaming orders and encouragement. Amid the incessant crash of rifle fire, the howls, shrieks and thundered blasphemies, his deafness was lost, his dour reserve forgotten. Chard, too, had acquired a carbine, and blazed into the surging enemy from a gap in the firing line. As the redcoats thrust down at the forest of assegais across the breastwork, Dabulamanzi's warriors snatched at the rifle barrels. It was a standing complaint of the British soldier that the barrel of his Martini-Henry became too hot to handle when fired rapidly. Now, he gave thanks for the circumstance.

By six o'clock, Dabulamanzi's temper had become strained. It was five full days since his regiments had left the barracks at Nodwengu, and the last two nights had been spent in the open with little food. His brief for the action at Isandhlwana had been merely to cut the track to Rorke's Drift, and this he had already exceeded by marching to the border, not to mention his further breach of orders by crossing the Buffalo. At the time, it had seemed a small infringement – a chance to mop up a few isolated enemy soldiers before retiring in good order to boast his success in the home kraals. But his plan had gone sour on him. Now, to compound his disobedience, he had serious losses to answer for. Worse, his chosen victims were still defying him.

Dabulamanzi was in a cleft stick. To delay returning his regiments would increase his culpability; to return them mauled, without victory, would be to face not only censure but ignominy. In this dilemma, he eschewed the course most likely to have doomed the outpost: i.e., to rest his men until dusk, then swamp the station with a mass attack by reorganised and refreshed regiments in the dim light. Instead, determined to speed the end at all costs, he flung his tiring warriors forward unimaginatively, without respite.

It cannot, at the time, have seemed much of a favour to the defenders. As the enemy continued to press by the thousand, oblivious of his mounting losses, it became evident to the slender company in the enclave that the larger perimeter was becoming untenable. To the west, the incomplete defences in front of the hospital were in immediate danger of falling. Hastily separating the area ahead of the hospital from the main compound with an ancillary barrier of mealie bags, Chard and Bromhead closed their men to the right along the original wall, now covering the hospital front by fire only. This strengthened the defenders to the centre-front of the perimeter, but also presented more targets to the Zulu marksmen firing into the back of this section, over the rear wall, from the Oskarberg. It could be a matter of very little time before continued survival depended upon the abandon-

Top The *koppie* at Isandhlwana.
The National Army Museum

Bottom Warriors enlisted with the British force in
Zululand.
The National Army Museum

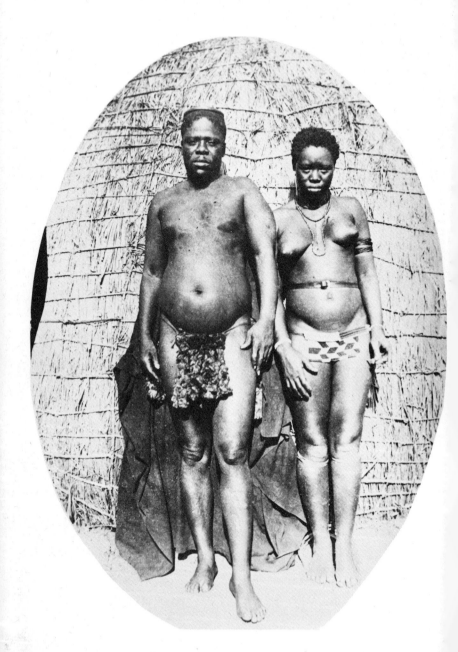

The Zulu captain Usibebu and his wife.
The South African Government Archives

Top left Lieut. Teignmouth Melville, V.C.

Top right Lieut. Gonville Bromhead, V.C.

Right Lieut. Nevill Coghill, V.C.

The Regimental Museum of the South Wales Borderers.

Top left Corporal William Allan,
V.C.

Top right Private William
Jones, V.C.

Right Private Henry Hook, V.C.

*The Regimental Museum of the
South Wales Borderers*

Top left Lieut. John Chard, R.E.

Top centre Colonel Anthony Durnford, R.E.

Top right Captain Charles Cavaye

Above left Captain Reginald Younghusband

Above centre Captain William Mostyn

Left Lieut. Charles D'A Pope

The Regimental Museum of the South Wales Borderers

Sequlequelee

The Zulu captain Sigcwelegcwele. Sketch by
E. Hutton.
The Johannesburg Africana Museum

one of Woods irregulars
(Swazies)

A Swazi tribesman. From the sketchbook of
Major John North Crealock.
The Regimental Museum of the Sherwood Foresters

Top Rorke's Drift. A reconstruction by Lady Butler, looking towards the storehouse and redoubt. Standing, centre, are Chard and Bromhead. Behind them, the artist has painted the bearded missionary Smith, who was mistakenly reported to have figured in the engagement.

By gracious permission of H.M. the Queen

Centre Defenders of Rorke's Drift. A group photograph of the survivors of the 24th Regiment taken shortly after the action.

The Radio Times Hulton Picture Library

ment of the main enclave and withdrawal to the small eastern compound incorporating the store house.

The pressure on the west raised an agonising problem. 'All this time,' Chard wrote later in his report, 'the enemy had been attempting to force the hospital, and shortly after, set fire to its roof. The garrison of the hospital defended it room by room.'

There were less than a dozen able-bodied men in the hospital, and any idea of a relief force from the critically-pressed perimeter was unthinkable. Those of the patients fit enough to stand and use a rifle had already joined the defenders. Others, in two rooms with access (via a window in the east wall of the hospital) to the main enclave, had been evacuated as the company began to withdraw towards the store-house compound. There remained thirteen patients in two rooms on the south and west of the hospital whose only access was directly into the Zulu mass outside the perimeter, or via a front verandah into that part of it now abandoned.

The west (left) wall of the hospital contained a single door; the south (rear) wall, three doors. All these were in imminent danger of being breached by squads of Zulus who had rushed the walls and established themselves sufficiently close to be impervious to fire from the loopholes. In a small room behind the door on the west wall, seven men were in a dire predicament, for they had no communication whatsoever with the rest of the building. At two loopholes stood Privates John and Joseph Williams of the 24th. They were unrelated. In fact, John, the son of a Welsh policeman, was serving under an assumed name. His true patronym was Fielding. With them were five patients, four bedridden, one capable of hobbling.

Their only conceivable hope of escape, as the Zulus smashed at the door, was through an inner wall into the next room. Snatching a pickaxe which had been used to make the loopholes, John Williams hacked at the substantial partition.

While he worked, the semi-mobile patient took his rifle and joined Joseph Williams at the loopholes. John had made the hole just large enough to squeeze through, and had managed to haul two of the helpless patients into the inner room, when the door gave. Joseph emptied his rifle into the oncoming warriors, then plunged his bayonet into the first to enter. The rest were on him before he could do more. Dragged outside, he was held down and his body shredded by assegais. The three patients still in the outer room perished with him.

John Williams and the two surviving patients were now in a larger room fronted by the verandah, which swarmed with Zulus. To the rear was a door leading to a back room containing eight more patients and another loophole guard, Private Henry Hook of Gloucestershire. Williams and his charges joined them. Again, they were trapped without egress. The Zulus were trying to break in from the verandah. They had also gained the room to the west and were attempting to force the intervening door. As before, the only hope of escape was by hacking through the eastern partition wall. Grimly, Williams set to work with his pickaxe. The rasp of the axe on stone was punctuated by shattering reports as Hook pumped bullets through the far door to discourage the warriors behind it.

This time, Williams managed to drag all the sick men through his rough tunnel before the door collapsed. Hook waited long enough to transfix the leading Zulu with his bayonet, then dived through the hole to safety.

Once more, the refuge was temporary.

Williams had emerged into the central room on the back wall of the hospital to find it occupied by a single soldier, a walking patient named Waters, who was firing desperately through a loophole to keep the marauders away from a door which gave directly to the outside. The door was the only outlet the room contained. For the third time, Williams hefted his axe in blistered hands and belaboured the eastern partition. There was now an additional note of urgency. The thatched roof was ablaze, and the heat and smoke were becoming menacing. It took him fifteen minutes to make the escape hole, another twenty to get the patients through. During this painful operation, Waters held to the loophole while Hook slotted low shots at the Zulus through the previous escape hole.

The fugitives were now in a long chamber with freeway to

the most easterly room and the window on to the main enclave. These rooms were defended by two Welshmen, Privates Robert and William Jones, unrelated but both recruited to the 24th from the expatriate labour force in Birmingham. The Joneses had already evacuated the sick from the end rooms, with the exception of a delirious sergeant, who refused to co-operate. Their news was not comforting. Chard and Bromhead had been forced to retire the company to the store-house compound, thirty yards to the east of the hospital. Their fire was holding the enemy from the intervening ground, now lit in the gathering darkness by the flaming roof, but the Zulus had possession of the rear barricade and were shooting in, and making sudden forays. There was no option but to run the gauntlet, humping the sick men.

Assisted by two redcoats on the outer wall – Corporal William Allan and Private Frederick Hitch, both of whom, though severely wounded, had stayed to help the evacuation – the sick men slid, or were pushed through the window, and were supported as best possible across the glowing no-man's-land. Of the twelve patients assembled for the final bid, ten were brought alive to the defended compound. One attempting to cross unaided, was jumped by a Zulu and assegai'd. The delirious sergeant had frustrated all efforts to remove him from the hospital. When Robert Jones braved the blazing building for a final attempt, it was too late. The enemy had broken in and butchered the sick man.

Towards dusk, the flames from the burning hospital had been visible far west. Major Spalding, riding ahead of the reserve company he had gone to fetch, saw the blaze and concluded, with alarm, that the outpost had been razed. Ahead, he could discern a strong body of Zulus. Galloping back to his column, he turned it about and hastened back to reinforce Helpmakaar. Dabulamanzi was scarcely happier. The garrison was tightly established in the compound, his main endeavours were spent, and he had nothing to show but mounting losses. Stubbornly, he kept the offensive boiling by the light of the burning thatch. Despite his warriors' dislike of night fighting, six distinct attacks were launched after dark. But the spirit as well as the energy of the regiments was waning, and each surge which spent itself on the stronghold weakened the resolution of the next.

Inside the compound, the defenders were grimed, bloody and exhausted, but serious casualties had been remarkably light. Surgeon Major Reynolds was probing, stitching and bandaging effectively. Many of the wounded, patched up, were still fighting. By midnight, the attack had subsided sufficiently for Chard to lead a sally beyond the breastworks to recover a watercart, from which the defenders gratefully slaked their thirst. In the early hours of the morning, the onslaught petered out. By daylight, the only Zulus in evidence were the scores of dead left behind by the frustrated regiments. Cautiously, a detail stepped over the corpses to the cookhouse. There was hot tea before breakfast.

Chapter Seven

NOT GUILTY,
BUT...

ఆ**ઠ✦ઠ**ૐ

Or to some coffee-house I stray,
For news, the manna of a day,
And from the hipp'd discourses gather
That politics go by the weather.

Matthew Green,
'The Spleen'

CHELMSFORD started west from Isandhlwana at the first glimmer
of daylight with what remained of the centre column. There
was nothing to be gained from letting the ranks examine the
ghastly scene of the ravaged camp – soldiers were best not
reminded that the banners of war concealed a stinking *abattoir* –
and much to be lost by lingering in Zululand without rations
and reserve ammunition. The general's anxiety to extricate his
force from Cetshwayo's kingdom at all haste was matched only
by the fear of what fresh horrors he might find to his rear.
The glow from the burning hospital at Rorke's Drift had been
clearly visible in the night at Isandhlwana, and the apprehension
of a Zulu invasion of Natal had not eased the chill hours of
darkness.

As the dejected troops trudged forebodingly back past Sirayo's
kraal, the scene of their first enthusiastic depredations, Dabulamanzi and his tattered regiments appeared to their left, slogging
home on a reverse path. The armies eyed each other glassily.

They were within hailing distance, but neither had the stomach for fresh battle. The bizarre encounter, combined with the finger of black smoke rising ahead from the valley of the Buffalo, increased the pessimism of the British force. Sombrely, the general sent a mounted patrol to scout the position at Rorke's Drift.

A faint burst of cheering beyond the river informed him that the outpost was still in friendly hands. It was 8 am. Cantering forward, Chelmsford encountered the second spectacle of wholesale death he had witnessed in a few hours. The first evidence was in the stream itself. Before retiring, Dabulamanzi's warriors had dragged scores of corpses to the river and pitched them into the current. Some had drifted back to the bank, or were caught on rocks. More were in the bush, and among boulders, beside the track, where the gravely wounded had expired beyond the scene of combat. Around the mission station itself, the carnage was formidable. Almost 400 Zulu bodies were sprawled against the barricades, or on the adjacent ground. The defenders had been out at dawn despatching those which had showed the last signs of life.

No less incredible, in the light of Isandhlwana, was the count of British casualties. A mere fifteen had died, including the sick who had perished in the hospital, and twelve men were wounded. Of the great majority who remained unscathed, many now lay in the sun in their shirtsleeves, sleeping off the shock and exhaustion. Some were puffing pipes. Private Hook was cooking breakfast. At least one was writing a letter.

The contrast between the two actions, fought within ten miles of each other on the same day, was too remarkable to go unnoticed. At Isandhlwana, the British force was outnumbered 9 to 1 by the Zulus (discounting Dabulamanzi's regiments); at Rorke's Drift, by 30 to 1. Yet Isandhlwana fell while Rorke's Drift beat off the attack. The comparative losses were even more striking. If one accepts the normal estimates of 2,000 Zulu dead at Isandhlwana, and 500 at Rorke's Drift, then for every 3 members of the British force who died at Isandhlwana 4 Zulus were killed, while for every 3 British who died at Rorke's Drift no less than a hundred Zulus were killed. Well over three-quarters of the defenders were lost at Isandhlwana; only a ninth of those at the outpost.

The reasons for such disparity could not be found in the behaviour of the enemy. In both actions, the Zulus employed the same simple encircling stratagem, attacking *en masse* with no great sophistication but extraordinary courage. Rorke's Drift proved that a company of steady, rifle-armed infantry could repel 4,000 Zulus – with a number of basic provisos: 1) a compact fighting formation; 2) a rudimentary breastwork, or laager, to fight behind; 3) a ready supply of ammunition. The first two of these conditions had been underlined repeatedly by the Boers; the third was elementary. The conclusion was inescapable. The difference between the greater disaster of Isandhlwana and the lesser triumph of Rorke's Drift was that a couple of not particularly brilliant lieutenants had taken the fundamental precautions neglected by their superiors.

While the tragic fiasco of Isandhlwana did not lack reverberations, Rorke's Drift saved the face of the imperial army and the image of the redoubtable redcoat. Quickly acclaimed an epic feat of British arms, the heroic defence not only helped to exorcise Isandhlwana from national memory, but went on to become the very stuff of folklore, sustained from generation to generation in martial reminiscence and the mass media. Perhaps no action of such trifling scale and strategic insignificance was ever exalted by so many high awards.

Eleven Victoria Crosses were bestowed upon the men of the outpost, seven of them within the single company of the 24th – almost one for every ten participants. Apart from Chard and Bromhead, the medals went to Reynolds, Dalton, Allan, Hitch, John Williams, Hook, William and Robert Jones, and a Corporal Friederich Schiess of the NNC, who had left his sick bed in the hospital to fight at the barricades. There might have been more had the VC been awarded, at that time, posthumously.

Both Chard and Bromhead were invited to a personal audience with Queen Victoria and belatedly promoted, not one rank but two, to brevet-major. Accountably, Bromhead's deafness promptly ceased to exercise his superiors. He served for a further thirteen years.

Nevertheless, the acclamation of Rorke's Drift could not immediately erase the accompanying débâcle. In Natal, there was near panic. For several days, the Zulu army was expected to sweep south at any hour. The whites retreated from the border, and every available settler was summoned to bear arms. Chelmsford, stopping at Helpmakaar long enough to convene a court of inquiry into Isandhlwana, hastened to Pietermaritzburg, where he made plans for the defence of the larger towns. When the Zulus showed no signs of avenging the British invasion, the colonies calmed down.

Chelmsford himself displayed no excitability. The qualities which made for an uninspiring leader, gave him an inscrutable and dignified presence in adversity. He seems to have been genuinely unreproachful of his generalship, and, perhaps more commendably, undisposed to lay blame on his subordinates. The court of inquiry was hardly penetrating. Of three key witnesses, two – Browne, who had had a unique overall view of the engagement, and Raw, the only surviving officer engaged on the Nqutu – were not called to give evidence. The third, Harness, whose artillery had been ordered to desist in its rescue bid, was disqualified from testifying as a member of the presiding board. Those survivors who did give evidence were understandably confused and disjointed in their recollections. The court recorded their testimony, but offered no opinion on the disaster. Chelmsford supported its reticence. The result of the action at Isandhlwana, he reported to London from Pietermaritzburg on the 27th, was beyond his understanding.

Others were less diffident. From first to last, they said, the handling of the centre column had been a saga of incompetence. Having neglected to laager his camp, Chelmsford had marched half its strength off on a wild goose chase to the distant hills without ascertaining that the Zulu army was already waiting with leisurely impunity on the near plateau. He had failed to scout adequately, he had failed to divide the responsibility for command sensibly (i.e., by leaving Glyn at Isandhlwana) and, even when advised that attack was imminent, had failed to take the action which yet could have saved the camp. Even the news that it had fallen had not immediately shaken his complacency.

Chelmsford's staff, by no means as aloof as the general, employed attack as the best means of defending virtue. Their main target was Durnford. The general's orders on leaving camp, his staff maintained, had been for the purely defensive use of those left behind. By over-reaching those orders, and initiating an unauthorised offensive, Durnford had weakened the camp and made its overthrow possible. The exploitation of Durnford as a scapegoat was rendered doubly repugnant in view of his brave death. Among those infuriated by the attack on his behaviour was his brother Edward, a retired colonel. Durnford, he pointed out, had been given no orders regarding his action or responsibility on reaching Isandhlwana. He could not be held accountable for orders issued to Pulleine, and had acted reasonably as an independent agent. Edward Durnford criticised Chelmsford bitterly.

The news of Isandhlwana reached Sir Michael Hicks Beach late on 11 February, and was common currency in England on the 12th. The consternation was not diminished by the fact that the shock came, as it where, from nowhere. Few Englishmen could have placed Zululand on a map, and the invasion had roused little interest. From a military viewpoint, all eyes were on Afghanistan, a flashpoint at once more familiar and significant, involving, as it did, the relationship with Russia. Frere's adventuring had already overstrained the war budget, and the last thing the Government wanted was any further trouble in South Africa. Disraeli, overwhelmed by the tidings, was obliged to retire to bed. The Queen took the news, if grimly, with stoicism, sending a message to Chelmsford, via the Secretary for War, expressing her 'confidence in the Commander-in-Chief and her troops to maintain her name and honour'.

That the nation did not share Her Majesty's sentiments towards Chelmsford was evident even in the House of Lords, where some sharp dissent moved Disraeli, now recovered from the initial shock, to explain that the message was not 'a formal expression of *unlimited* confidence'.

The Zulu War

If this did little to placate the general's critics, the cabinet's reaction to the situation did less. Instead of superseding Chelmsford and reviewing the whole position in south-east Africa, it resolved on a radical increase of the forces assigned to him. The 57th Foot, the West Middlesex Regiment, was ordered to sail from Ceylon, a requisition for all disposable troops was telegraphed to Bombay, and seven infantry regiments in England, plus two of cavalry, with additional artillery and engineers, were warned for immediate service in South Africa. The clamour against Chelmsford, Frere, and indeed the war itself, intensified.

In the House of Commons, the Government was strongly pressed to recall Chelmsford. When Sir Stafford Northcote, secretary to the Chancellor of the Exchequer, declared that the Government had no intention of placing the supreme command in South Africa in other hands, Sir Robert Peel, member for Tamworth, proposed the adjournment of the House. In the confusion which followed, Chelmsford was accused of gross military incapacity, the Horse Guards was berated as a hotbed of intrigue, and the Queen and Court were charged with shielding incompetence. Peel wished to know if the inadequacy of the Commander-in-Chief and the consequent Zulu victory, was a proper reason for continuing the war. It was left to Lord Hartington, Liberal leader in the Commons, to cool things down by suggesting that it might be better to await more military information before censuring the conduct of the campaign. At last, the motion was withdrawn.

Opposition to the war gained appreciably by the publication of a dispatch from Hicks Beach to Sir Bartle Frere. In this document, the High Commissioner was upbraided in no uncertain terms for his provocation of Cetshwayo – for 'taking without full knowledge and sanction a course almost certain to result in war, which, as I had previously impressed on you, every effort should have been taken to avoid'. The Government, added Hicks Beach, would not recall the High Commissioner, but trusted 'there would be no recurrence of any cause for complaint on this score'.

On 25 March, Lord Lansdowne, a former Under-Secretary for War, brought a motion in the Lords regretting that, in view of the Colonial Secretary's censure, the conduct of affairs in South

Africa should remain in Frere's hands. Some steam was removed from the debate by the Government's failure to make much of a defence for the High Commissioner. He had, admitted Lord Cranbrook, made a mistake in doing something they would rather he had not done, but he had done it from a sense of duty and should be corrected moderately. It was the Government's purpose, his lordship reminded the chamber, to bring about a scheme of confederation in South Africa (first proposed by the former Under-Secretary for the Colonies, Lord Carnarvon). There was, Cranbrook asserted, a perpetual danger in that area from Zululand. It was simply not possible to ignore it.

At the division, the Government emerged with 156 votes to 61, but abstentions were heavy and the figures scarcely represented the warmth of feeling in the country. Two days later, the vigorous and influential Sir Charles Dilke put an identical motion to the Commons. Arraigning the whole of Frere's policy, Dilke accused him of deliberately wrecking a peaceful co-existence with Zululand which had endured for thirty years. Time and again, Frere's dispatches had clearly indicated his intention of committing offensive and aggressive acts against that nation, yet the Government had been content passively to acknowledge such missives. From 23 January to 19 March, no word of censure had been addressed to him on his breach of government direction. In full knowledge of the Government's views regarding the war he was planning, Dilke said, Frere appeared to have calculated that if he gained a triumphant victory and added a new province to the British Empire, all his transgressions would be overlooked.

Doubtless, observed Dilke, many now challenged the High Commissioner simply on his failure, but if the authority of government meant anything then he deserved to be challenged regardless of the outcome of his enterprise.

Northcote defended Frere somewhat faint-heartedly, while Hicks Beach, in some contortions, denied that government policy had been inconsistent with that of the High Commissioner. The matter, he declared, was simply one of excessive zeal. It was left to Sir William Harcourt, Liberal member for Derby, to sum up the Government's attitude to Frere most succinctly. The verdict, he suggested laconically, was 'Not guilty – but don't do it again!' Though the point was well taken, it did not shatter loyalties. The censure was defeated by 60 votes. The Government, having rebuked Frere, had joined his war.

✿

Chelmsford had retired to Natal soundly beaten, but at least the remnants of his column were now safe. Two invading forces, on the other hand, still remained in Zululand. Colonel Charles Pearson and his right column had crossed the Tugela at the Lower Drift on 12 January, heading for the deserted mission station of Eshowe, across the coastal lands, which was schemed as his first main base on the march to Ulundi.

Pearson, a handsome, heavy-jowled officer whose doughty appearance well reflected the reputation of his regiment, the 3rd Foot, the East Kent ('Buffs'), was methodical by nature, not given to taking risks. His invasion camp on the Natal bank of the Tugela, sited on a high spur overlooking the river, had been protected by a stout outer earthwork which gave it the appearance of some great stronghold cleft to the landscape by Iron Age man. From an inner compound, he had sited his artillery to command the far bank, on which, having made his crossing, he spent the best part of a week constructing a further defensive post with tall earth walls capable of holding the entire column. These bulwarks, known as Fort Pearson and Fort Tenedos – the second after HMS *Tenedos*, a naval vessel supporting the column – solidly illustrated the contrast between Pearson's approach and Chelmsford's.

The strength of Pearson's column approximated to that of the central column at its outset. The backbone of the force was two battalions of imperial infantry, one of the colonel's own regiment under a Colonel Henry Parnell, the other of the 99th Foot, the Duke of Edinburgh's Lanarkshire, commanded by Colonel William Welman. There was also a body of about 200 seamen and marines which brought two seven-pounders and a Gatling to strengthen a Royal Artillery contingent with two field pieces and a rocket battery.

Of irregulars, Pearson commanded two battalions of the NNC under another East Kent officer, Major Shapland Graves, and two hundred cavalry of the Durban, Stranger, Victoria and Alexandra Rifles. This horse troop, supplemented by 100 mounted British infantry, was led by a regular cavalry officer, Major Percy Barrow of the 19th Hussars.

Unlike the centre column, the right column achieved the river crossing with a minimum of drama. One man fell from a pontoon and was snapped up by a crocodile, otherwise the exercise was exemplary. On the morning of the 18th, Pearson started for Eshowe with five companies of the East Kent, the naval contingent, half the levies and cavalry, the artillery and fifty wagons. Welman followed next day with the rest of the command and eighty wagons. The trail led through low, alluvial land, often marshy, across which numerous small rivers coursed towards the near sea. Pearson advanced with circumspection, scouting systematically. When the wagons dropped behind, he halted until they caught up. On the 21st, he detached a body of infantry to investigate a military kraal to the east. The kraal, named Gingindhlovu (the British dubbed it Gin-Gin-I-love-you), was deserted. The infantry burned it.

On the morning of the 22nd, the column breakfasted beyond the river, the Inyezane, in preparation for a climb ahead. About three-quarters of a mile from the Inyezane, the terrain shelved upwards to a plateau on which Eshowe was located. Facing Pearson were three spurs of rising land, up the centre of which ran the path he was following. From the two valleys between the outer spurs and the centre spur, a couple of small streams filtered down to the Inyezane, one on either flank of the column. The troops were still resting in the bush between these water-courses when a scouting party of Zulus appeared on the skyline surmounting the spurs, a height known as Majia's hill.

Pearson ordered a company of levies forward to dislodge the Zulu scouts. The levies started up the central spur to the front of the column, but, as they approached, the enemy party shifted to the top of the right spur. Veering into the intervening valley, the Kaffirs began to climb towards the skulking Zulus. They had gained the right ridge, and were about 400 yards short of their quarry, when hundreds of warriors topped the rise ahead and streamed down the spur at them. For a moment, there was confusion. Then the levies were swept back into the valley, leaving two European officers and six men dead, while the Zulus continued to descend towards the column's flank.

Cunningly using the furled hills to escape Pearson's observations, a veteran Zulu captain named Umatyiya had worked several thousand warriors (including the iQwa, inGulube and umXapho, which had not yet met the British) into the region of Majia's hill, under orders from Cetshwayo to stop the British column. The advancing levies had forced Umatyiya to attack prematurely. One horn was now precipitated down the right spur, while the other had yet to reach the top of the left spur.

Pearson's reaction was precise and provident. Deploying the bulk of his irregulars defensively to each side of the track, facing on to the two streams, he dashed his artillery forward on to a commanding knoll at the foot of the centre spur and surrounded it with infantry and navy men. The field pieces were unlimbered and trained in record time. From this natural gun platform, the Zulus swarming down the right ridge were subjected to a devastating barrage of shell, rockets and rifle fire. The majority of the warriors turned back. Some had reached the bush at the bottom, and spread along the British flank. Welman, who had brought his force up behind Pearson, swept into these from the rear of the column and they scattered rapidly.

Umatyiya's men rallied at the top of the centre spur, crowding a small kraal there and working round on to the left ridge. Redirecting his artillery fire on to the kraal, Pearson sent the naval contingent, backed by a company of East Kent, to seize it. Behind them stumbled the crew of the Gatling, manhandling the cumbersome ten-barrelled weapon, in charge of an eighteen-year-old midshipman, Lewis Coker. By the time Coker reached the summit, the kraal had been taken by the British. The Zulus spreading down the left spur were hesitant. His men laid the gun and started cranking. It swept the slopes with promiscuous deadliness. Ninety minutes after the first sighting of the Zulus, they were gone, their killed and wounded carried with them. About 300 warriors had died in the action from a number of regiments. The wounded were more numerous.

Pearson's men resumed the march with new confidence. They had met the legendary enemy and hammered him from open column. After the initial NNC loss of eight men, only two more had been killed and sixteen wounded. Two officers, Pearson himself and Parnell, had had their horses shot from under them. The odds were far from unacceptable. It looked, observed one officer, like being an easy war. Pearson climbed four miles beyond the Inyezane and camped on a defensible ridge near running water.

Next day, the column reached the old mission station at Eshowe. The scrub had encroached on the grounds, but the deserted buildings – a church, a school and a dwelling house – were in good repair. The elevated situation, skirted by dumpy hills and bosky slopes, offered majestic vistas of the south-east of Cetshwayo's kingdom. From a near rise, the eye could follow the Inyezane east to the shimmer that was the Indian Ocean, twenty miles away. A few miles farther to the south, across half a dozen rivers, the mound of Fort Pearson could be seen standing guard on the Tugela.

Pearson did not linger to admire the view. Like his men, he had been bucked by the Inyezane action, but he was not complacent. As soon as the tents were pitched at Eshowe, he had the troops digging trenches round them, and his engineers planning fortifications to embrace the whole station. His caution was quickly justified. Two days after arriving at the mission, word arrived from the Tugela of some sort of set-back to the central column. The details were not clear. Durnford, it appeared, had been killed, and his native troops massacred, but where the engagement had taken place was not specified. In itself, the message was less than momentous. Durnford's force had not been large, neither was the defeat of levies deemed too significant.

But there were disturbing concurrences. A further message indicated that Fort Tenedos had been attacked. The enemy had been repulsed, and there were no losses. Nevertheless, linked with the reported fate of Durnford, whom Pearson still regarded as the commander at Middle Drift, it concentrated attention uncomfortably on communications. Patrols riding in from the south added to Pearson's uneasiness with news of a proliferation of small Zulu war-parties between Eshowe and the Tugela. On the morning of the 28th, an extraordinary communication arrived from Chelmsford, datelined Pietermaritzburg.

> Consider all my instructions as cancelled and act in whatever manner you think most desirable in the interests of the column under your command. Should you consider the garrison at Eshowe as too far advanced to be fed with safety, you can withdraw it. Hold, however, if possible, the post on the Zulu side of the Tugela. You must be prepared to have the whole Zulu force down upon you. Do away with tents, and let the men take shelter under the wagons, which will then be in position for defence and hold so many more supplies.

Perhaps the most remarkable aspect of this singular directive was its lack of information. In a few sketchy words – they might have been composed in the last minutes of Isandhlwana rather than from the safety of Pietermaritzburg – Chelmsford revoked his whole briefing for the campaign, talked about holding the border rather than advancing on Ulundi, and hinted that Pearson was the target for a mass assault. With this, there was not a word of explanation. Pearson was to act in any way he thought 'most desirable'. But by what criteria was he to judge what was most desirable when he had no idea what had happened, where the rest of the invasion forces were sited, and why the general had changed his plans?

Had the message been designed to convey the maximum of misgivings with the minimum of helpfulness, it could hardly have been more successful. Plainly, something entirely unexpected had happened. For the rest, Pearson had little more than his imagination to fall back on. It was an attribute he was too old a campaigner to trust with any happiness.

The extent of his perplexity is illustrated by the unorthodoxy of his reaction. While the men continued to labour at Eshowe's defences beneath the fierce sun, Pearson called an emergency council among his officers and took a vote on what to do next. The overwhelming decision – resting largely on the inadequacy of supplies should they be besieged – was to withdraw to the Tugela. Soon afterwards, however, seventy wagons loaded with supplies and ammunition, and escorted by five companies of infantry, pulled in from Fort Tenedos. By a narrow majority, the council revised its decision. Instead of a general withdrawal, it was now agreed to send back the mounted men and levies, to save food, and hold Eshowe with the remaining British troops. They were about 1,300 in number, and there was enough ammunition to provide 300 rounds apiece.

Far to the north of Pearson, across the breadth of Zululand, where great flat-topped ranges rose from the swampy headwater regions of the Blood River, the White and Black Umfolosi and the Pongola, the left column of Chelmsford's army, had been leading a mercurial existence. The hills here, in the disputed territories adjoining the Transvaal, abounded with Zulu clans, but of all Cetshwayo's subjects their link with Ulundi was the most tenuous. Many of the hill tribes were semi-autonomous. Accustomed to guarding their own lands, they had not sent their warriors to the royal army, and it was necessary for the column to test their allegiance before leaving them in its rear. For this reason, Chelmsford had allowed his left force a certain latitude in its movement.

Nothing could better have suited its commander. Lieutenant-Colonel Henry Evelyn Wood, VC, was a Wolseley protégé whose wide experience of active service had culminated in a 'special duties' assignment in Ashanti. In a later period, his characteristics might have commended him as a guerilla leader. He hardly looked like a regular officer. Fortyish, of slight, stunted physique, with thinning temples and a straggling moustache, he was a gnomish man with the long, wan features of a gentle goat. Wood had joined the services at fourteen, since when he had fought in the Crimea, the Indian Rebellion and Ashanti. He had won the VC in an action of characteristic initiative against an Indian bandit troop. Calculating, cerebral, a talented linguist, Wood was every-thing his cavalry commander was not.

Major Redvers Buller, who led the 200 Frontier Light Horse with the column, had, at forty, all the makings of an early Blimp. He was heavy, pompous and bad-tempered, with a theatrically martial bearing, a flabby chin and a loud voice. The fact that he was also a Wolseley protégé, evidenced the canny perceptiveness of Sir Garnet. For beneath Buller's bluster lay a fearless and uncomplicated approach to soldiering which com-municated itself to troops in the field more eloquently than the sophistry of brighter men.

The rest of the column comprised a battalion of the 13th Foot, the Somersetshire Light Infantry; a battalion of the 90th Foot, the Perthshire Volunteers Light Infantry; a body of mounted infantry; four seven-pounders and two rocket tubes; and several thousand Swazi levies, hereditary enemies of the Zulus.

Wood entered Zululand from the Transvaal via Utrecht, and was across the Blood River before the expiry of Frere's ultimatum. He had with him an old Boer farmer, Piet Uys, who had lost his father and brother fighting Zulus, and who knew his way about the northern territory. In a series of brisk marches, by night as well as day, Wood proceeded to crisscross the solitary, oddly haunting area. Gaunt cranes stalked in marsh mists. Snipe cried thinly overhead. Massive tabletops loomed from the headwaters like hippopotami. First, holding to the east of a long range named the Doornberg, he slipped south, taking a flying column with Uys and Buller to within twelve miles of Rorke's Drift. Retracing his steps, he encamped at Bembas Kop, an eminence across the Blood River from the north end of the Doornberg, covering the track to Utrecht. Here, swept by heavy rains, he stopped for five days.

When the ground had dried sufficiently to bear wagons, Wood was off again, this time east to the upper reaches of the White Umfolosi. Though Buller had spent the wet period scouting and rustling cattle, the column had yet to be opposed by the Zulus. The initial encounter, with a minor chief named Tinta, was encouraging. Tinta submitted peacefully. With his retainers, he was sent back to Utrecht under an infantry escort. Wood occupied his kraal.

A few miles distant, beyond the Umfolosi, lay two massive tabletops, separated by a narrow neck. The north-westerly of these heights (to the left, as Wood surveyed them) was Zunguin mountain; the south-westerly (to the right) was Hlobane mountain. Both were narrow, several miles long and guarded by rocky cliffs. They were natural strongholds, and Wood could not proceed south until they had been investigated. On 20 January, he sent Buller to scout with a mounted force. At the north of Zunguin, the riders were assailed by up to a thousand Zulus and forced to retire towards the river. Wood strengthened his camp and, on the 21st, planned the sort of operation in which he excelled. At midnight, he set out with his entire column to attain the mountains under cover of darkness.

As dawn illuminated Zunguin, the people of the abaQulusi, a tribe which grazed its cattle on the plateau, were amazed to see the British troops bearing down on them. Leaving their herd to the invaders, they disappeared into the morning mist, heading for the kraal of their chief, Msebe. Reaching the neck at the south end of the mountain, Wood looked across to the slopes of Hlobane. He was fascinated to discover about 4,000 Zulus at drill there. 'Their evolutions, which were plainly visible by the aid of a glass, were executed with ease and precision; a circle, a triangle and a hollow square, with a partition across it, being formed rapidly by movements of companies.'

Wood's column spent the day of Isandhlwana at rest in the shadow of the tabletops. It became increasingly apparent that Tinta's submission had not been a general precedent, and that the hill tribes would have to be suppressed before the colonel could think of drawing closer to Ulundi. This did not worry him. It was part of his mission to subdue the north. Moreover, he had learned from spies he had sent south that Cetshwayo's army was directed in force against the central column. Chelmsford would deal with that. He, Wood, had nothing to fear from that direction.

On the morning of the 24th, he advanced to disperse a body of Zulus on the far side of Hlobane, sending Buller on to the slopes to parry a couple of hundred warriors who were menacing his wagons. A somewhat tentative confrontation was developing, when a breathless native rode up to Wood with news of Chelmsford's disaster. The report, though not official, left no doubt that the invasion had misfired. If Cetshwayo had defeated the general, Wood could no longer regard himself as safe from the main Zulu army. He acted promptly. Ordering an immediate retreat to the Umfolosi, he started back briskly for the relative security of Tinta's kraal.

The column reached the kraal on the 25th, and Wood took rapid stock. There were no fuel supplies in the area, and the camp was not ideally defensible. Ten miles upstream, at a point known as Kambula hill, there was a stronger position, plentiful in fuel and drinking water. Kambula had another advantage. Directly between Zunguin mountain and Utrecht, and roughly equidistant from Utrecht and the border town of Luneberg, it would give better cover to the European settlements. They might be in dire need of it. Wood decided to move there. It took several days to shuttle his supplies up the river, each spent in apprehension of onslaught. The column had barely settled in the new camp, and begun to dig intrenchments, when word arrived from Chelmsford. The worst was confirmed at last. Wood could look for no help.

Chapter Eight

A
MITE
MORE TERROR

❧❀❧

*'The horror of that moment,' the King went
on, 'I shall never, never forget!' 'You
will though,' the Queen said, 'if you don't
make a memorandum of it.'*

Lewis Carroll,
Alice in Wonderland

FOR Cetshwayo, Isandhlwana was a tragic victory. Of the Zulu
losses, he declared: 'An assegai has been plunged into the nation's
belly. There are not enough tears to mourn the dead.' The king
had not wanted the battle, but it had been forced on him, and
the invader chastened. Honour had been served. Now the moment
seemed auspicious for a settlement. There was, however, the
problem, as the Zulu monarch saw it, of the surviving British
columns. Chelmsford, having been beaten, had withdrawn to his
own territory like any reasonable African general. Wood, lurk-
ing on the remote northern frontier, might yet be dismissed as
irresolute, a skulking hyena. Pearson was Cetshwayo's bogey-
man. An induna who fortified himself in the heart of enemy
country, and stuck there resolutely when his general was defeated,
had no antecedent in Zulu history.

Having chosen to fight his battle with the centre column,
Cetshwayo nourished hopes of halting Pearson by diplomacy.
From a European viewpoint, the idea of treating separately with

the columns was naïve; to the African mind, it was not. It is doubtful if the king realised that the three invading forces had an overall commander – certainly, at this stage, he did not know who it was. Already, he had sent eight messengers to the Lower Tugela to intimate his desire to talk terms, and not one had been returned to him. As a result, he had been obliged to instruct Umatyiya to delay Pearson as best he might.

'Regarding Inyezane,' concluded a border agent named Eustace Fanin, on the evidence of Zulu contacts, 'Cetshwayo contends that Colonel Pearson provoked the attack made on him by burning kraals and committing other acts of hostility along the line of march. He now asks that both sides should put aside their arms and resume negotiations with a view to a permanent settlement of all questions between himself and the (British) Government.' The king also begged, said Fanin, that his detained envoys be returned to him. 'I asked whether the Zulu army was still assembled. They say it is not; the men are all in their kraals.'

This was corroborated by intelligence gathered by the troops themselves. Even Dabulamanzi, whose royal blood had spared him the appropriate consequences of his Rorke's Drift adventure, had settled back on his homestead, not far from Eshowe – the focus of Cetshwayo's dilemma. To attack Eshowe would be to perpetuate hostilities he did not want, and incur further casualties the nation could not afford. On the other hand, to suffer an enemy garrison in the land was an intolerable indignity. Again, the king tried a pacific gesture. Under cover of a white flag, two royal ambassadors approached Eshowe to offer the column a safe passage back to the Tugela.

Pearson immediately clapped the messengers into irons, denouncing their mission as a crude trap. Yet there seems little reason to doubt the king's sincerity. His one wish was to be rid of the British troops – if at all possible, without the cruel losses he had learned to expect from further fighting.

It was a forlorn hope. Paradoxically, had the British aggressors triumphed at Isandhlwana, Cetshwayo might have stood a chance of salvaging the remnants of Zulu sovereignty from an ensuing peace. As it was, Chelmsford's defeat had sealed the doom of the nation. Already, the reinforcements on their way from England far outnumbered the total force with which the general had invaded Zululand. From the ashes of Isandhlwana would rise a monster of vengeance against which all the valour and sacrifice of the embattled African kingdom must prove futile. But that was in the future. The white captains were not yet transcendent.

With the defences complete at Kambula, and no concerted hostile action evident from the northern Zulu clans, Wood began to reassert his initiative. His endeavours, increasingly ambitious, took two forms: firstly, the procurement of defections from Cetshwayo's authority among the independently-minded chiefs of the area; and secondly, the harassment of the loyalists with a view to the same end. He also gave some assistance to the British reserve column on the Transvaal frontier, which, under Colonel Roberts, was operating out of Luneberg against bands of freebooting Zulus and Swazis on the eastern Transvaal border.

In the aggressive part of this programme, Buller was indefatigable. On 1 February, with his Frontier Horse and the troop of Boers which accompanied Piet Uys, he rode thirty miles east to raid the kraal of the emaQulusini, a tribe rich in cattle and stored grain. Dashing headlong at the huts, the cavalry paused long enough to fire them, galloped on to the grazing grounds, rounded up 400 head of cattle, and rode off with them before the surprised Zulus could organise resistance. Before the second week of February was out, Buller had led two more raids towards the eastern mountains, ravaging and plundering. A further 500 beasts were driven in. So seldom was the beefy major seen dismounted, that camp legend held him to sleep in his saddle.

On the 14th, in conjunction with Uys and a force from Luneberg, Buller set off through the mountains by night to attack the joint base of a minor Zulu chief named Manyanyoba and a Swazi bandit, Mbilini, whose depredations in the Intombe valley, to the rear of Luneberg, threatened the communications between that place and Derby, in the Transvaal. Buller took with him a single field piece, which, its wheels muffled in raw-hide, was trundled into place by moonlight, ready to fire into the bandit kraal when dawn broke. The second shell burst in the very centre of the clustered huts, creating the wildest confusion as flames and thick smoke engulfed the dry roofs.

As Buller's cavalry charged into the community, the stunned warriors stood to fire a ragged volley of musketry, then fled into the nearby hills. Thirty-four were killed before reaching safety, against three dead and three wounded in Buller's force. He returned with several hundred head of cattle, plus two large flocks of sheep and goats, having been in the saddle no less than nine hours.

Meanwhile, Wood, complementing Buller's brawn with his own restless guile, was deploying blandishments against one of the major chiefs of the north, a hugely fat man named Uhamu who was reputed to govern about 6,000 Zulus. Uhamu, a half-brother of Cetshwayo, was a self-indulgent ruler with an eye for the main chance. This, he nervously concluded after some weeks of vacillation, lay in joining the British. By mid-March, he was at Kambula, arranging for his 300 wives and countless children to follow him. Far from all of Uhamu's people subscribed to his desertion of the national cause – indeed, some of the loyalists fell upon the defectors with spears as they moved out – but the king's half-brother was a distinct step up from Tinta, and Wood made the most of the propaganda.

At the same time, he had assumed command of all troops in the Luneberg and Derby districts, including, among a number of non-Boer volunteers, the Kaffrarian Rifles, a corps raised among survivors and descendants of a German community settled in British Kaffraria after the Crimean War. The hostility of the Transvaal Boers towards British rule was fast becoming a new physical force in South Africa, and Colonel Roberts, alerted to a strong armed muster for Kruger near Pretoria, had been obliged to leave the frontier. Luneberg was now garrisoned by five slender companies of the 80th Foot, the Staffordshire Volunteers, under Major Charles Tucker. On 7 March, one of these companies was detached into the trouble-ridden Intombe valley to meet and escort a column of supply wagons approaching from Derby. It was against this background that Wood's burgeoning success was reversed by the first of two savage blows.

The escort company, about 100 strong under Captain David Moriarty, a middle-aged Irishman who had served in the Hazara campaign of 1868, but who had spent several of the intervening years on half pay, had marched no more than a mile or two north of Luneberg when it saw the first part of the wagon train halted on the far bank of the Intombe, unable to cross the drift there due to the swirling waters, flooded by recent rain. The river, fifty yards wide, was still rising.

By the use of an improvised raft, two of the wagons were ferried to the south bank while Moriarty, with the bulk of his company, having crossed to the far side by the same method, continued north to meet the rest of the supply train. None of the wagons was missing, but some had been plundered, and the jittery drivers reported Mbilini's and Manyanyoba's marauders operating in the vicinity. Moriarty had shepherded the whole column to the north side of the drift by the afternoon of the 9th, but the river was now a torrent, and any idea of ferrying more vehicles had to be discounted until the current subsided. On the 11th, Tucker, worried by the non-appearance of the wagon train, rode out of Luneberg to discover what had happened.

He found some thirty of Moriarty's bayonets camped on the south bank of the Intombe beside the two wagons which had crossed, and the remainder of the wagons and troops with Moriarty on the north bank. The captain had formed the vehicles into a V-shaped laager pointing back towards Derby, its open side covered by the river. The ammunition wagons and oxen were disposed within the laager, while the tents of the seventy-odd infantrymen on that side of the water were in a space between the westerly side of the V and the river bank. Moriarty's own tent was outside the point of the laager, beside the track to Derby. The notion was sound, but the detail was wanting.

'Major Tucker,' ran an intelligence report compiled afterwards, 'on inspecting the arrangements for defence, considered the wagons too far apart, and objected to the space left between the last wagons of the laager and the river bank.' His objections, it seems, were not forceful ones. According to the same report, Tucker 'did not order any change to be made'.

When Tucker turned his horse back for Luneberg, the flow of water was easing and he visualised a crossing the next day. Moriarty and his men bedded down with the same thought. They were, as one put it, 'within a stone's throw of Luneberg', and none seems to have anticipated danger. Despite rising ground and thick bush in the area, no outlying pickets were posted, and only two sentries were on duty on the north bank, one each side of the laager. On the south side, a further two sentries stood guard for the detachment with the isolated wagons. It was one of the second pair who sensed trouble and turned out his companions. He had heard a shot, he told Lieutenant Henry Harward, the officer in charge of the detachment. The sound had come from the north.

It was about 4.30 am, still dark, the river wreathed in thick mist. Harward sent a message across to Moriarty to check that all was well on the north bank, and to report the shot. Moriarty noted the message, then seems to have returned to bed. About half an hour later, the first streaks of light in a cloudy sky, a crash of musketry broke from the surrounding bush and getting on for a thousand Zulus raced towards the sleeping camp. Moriarty, stumbling from his tent, barely had time to shout 'Guard, turn out!' before he was cut down by assegais. The few Staffordshire men and wagon drivers who escaped his fate hurled themselves into the river undressed, to become the targets for flying spears and musket fire.

On the south bank, Harward and his detachment watched dumbfounded through the rising mist. Throwing themselves behind their two wagons, they gave the swimming fugitives what cover they could by volleying at the dim shapes massed across the river. This assistance did not last long. Several hundred Zulus were already in the water, heading for the Luneberg shore, and Harward's men were soon struggling for their own lives. In the deadly mêlée which ensued, Harward managed to save his horse. Ordering his senior NCO, Colour Sergeant Anthony Booth, to try and make the shelter of a distant farmhouse with the survivors, he mounted and rode full-stretch for Luneberg and assistance. Booth started his retreat with eleven men. Falling back steadily, they responded with a burst of rifle fire whenever the Zulus swarmed in at them. A few stragglers from the north bank rallied to Booth's stand. He had lost four of his small band, and pursued his stubborn retreat for a long hour, before his attackers gave up and slipped away to the surrounding hills.

Tucker put 150 bayonets of the 80th on to the road to the Intombe the moment he heard Harward's news, and galloped ahead with a small party of mounted men. The Zulus had gone when he arrived at the river, as had every ox, every round of ammunition, every rifle, every object of value. Only the wagons remained – and the stripped and mutilated bodies of Moriarty and seventy-nine of his party. Mbilini and Manyanyoba had exacted a bloody price for the raid on their headquarters.

Sergeant Booth was awarded the VC for salvaging the remnants of the force from the massacre. Harward was later arraigned before a general court martial at Pietermaritzburg for abandoning his post in the face of the enemy. The court, taking note that he had possessed the only horse available, and that nothing but the most urgent assistance could save the situation, found him not guilty. The trial had a far-reaching sequel. While the Commander-in-Chief ordered Harward's release and return to duty, he expressed his aversion to the findings by marking the court's report 'disapproved and not confirmed'. Shortly afterwards, the following observations on the matter, drafted by Wolseley, were ordered to be read to every regiment in the British army:

The more helpless a position in which an officer finds his men, the more it is his bounden duty to stay and share their fortune, whether for good or ill. It is because the British officer has always done so that he possesses the influence he does in the ranks of our army. The soldier has learned to feel that, come what may, he can in the direst moment of danger look with implicit faith to his officer, knowing that he will never desert him under any possible circumstances.

It is to this faith of the British soldier in his officers that we owe most of the gallant deeds recorded in our military annals.

Be that as it might – and Sergeant Booth's VC was only the most immediate of many ironic comments on the last assertion – the next disaster cast no imputations on the bravery of the British officer, merely the more standard charge of impercipience.

The main drawback to effective operations against Mbilini and Manyanyoba was the body of Zulus on Hlobane mountain. Before the move to Kambula, Wood had stood on the tip of Zunguin, trained his glasses east across Zunguin Nek (the ground between the heights), and watched several thousand warriors drilling on Hlobane. Their presence had continued to worry him. So long as these militant clansmen, largely abaQulusi, remained perched above the territory, all major movements from Kambula were inhibited. When, towards the end of March, Chelmsford appealed for a diversionary move in the north to draw attention from Eshowe, Wood decided the time had come to clear Hlobane.

On 26 March, he summoned Buller and Uys to his tent and told them his intention. The Zulu defectors he had questioned deemed the mountain impregnable, but Wood had scouted it from the foot and believed there were two approaches to its flat top: one up a snaking path at the eastern end of its long south face, the other a steeper climb up the western extremity. Though more abrupt in ascent, the western end of the mountain was lower than the rest, a prominent step distinguishing it from the bulk of the plateau which was thus divided into two levels. Wood's plan was to launch a force up each end and squeeze the Zulus in the middle. As a bonus, he would capture the rich herd of cattle the abaQulusi grazed on the mountaintop.

The operation, somewhat euphemistically referred to in official reports as a reconnaissance, commenced the next day. Buller and Uys, with a force of rather less than 700, comprising 400 cavalry and a body of Natal foot levies, rode east beneath the south face of the eminence and bivouacked on the plain for the night in preparation for a dawn ascent of the twisting path to the higher eastern plateau. The force assigned to the lower western plateau similarly bivouacked beneath the heights, having completed the shorter march. Commanded by Major John Russell of the 12th Lancers, it comprised 250 horse, about 150 of Uhamu's defected Zulus and a further body of foot levies, in all about 640 men. Wood followed later with a small bodyguard, his staff (headed by Captain the Hon. Ronald Campbell, Coldstream Guards) and among others, Llewellyn Lloyd, a political agent.

The night passed depressingly with rain and thunder. Lightning provided cheerless glimpses of the wet cliffs, frightened the horses, and the men got little sleep. At 3.30 am, Buller abandoned the bivouac and pressed forward. The storm lashed him as he picked his way up the slippery, precipitous trail in the dark, his troopers frequently forced to dismount and scramble forward leading their animals. Daylight proved a mixed blessing. Now the footholds were visible, but so were the climbers to a throng of Zulu marksmen clustered in caves on the cliffs and crouched behind boulders. Buller was lucky to reach the top without worse losses than two officers, two men and a dozen horses. The storm had passed. There was soft grass underfoot again. Spreading his levies ahead in search for cattle, he began to move west towards Russell as pre-arranged.

Russell's force, making its ascent from Zunguin Nek, reached the lower western plateau unopposed and, also scouting for cattle, drove eastward. Wood, having waited to see it start its climb, had led his small party briskly across the plain, following the southern aspect of Hlobane, towards the base of the track up which Buller had fought his way.

Wood had covered about half the distance when he met a band of about sixty Border Horse, mostly English settlers organised and commanded by Colonel Frederick Weatherley, formerly 4th Light Dragoons, who had left the regular army to farm in the Transvaal. Riding with Weatherley was his son, a boy of fifteen. Since the Border Horse were supposed to be with Buller, Wood asked where they were going. Weatherley replied that they had got lost in the storm and were looking for Buller, a somewhat dubious explanation in view of the fact that they were riding in the opposite direction, back towards Kambula. Wood pointed to their error, and rode on with deprecations about fair-weather amateurs.

A ruddy sun was rising as his party reached the foot of Buller's path up the hillside, now marked by the dead troop horses, some shot, some killed in falls from the rocky cliff. As Wood and his staff began to toil up the incline, the Zulu snipers in the caves opened fire on them. Lloyd was hit and mortally wounded. The party fell back on Weatherley's troop, which had followed at some distance. Since it made no move when Wood ordered it forward to clear the path, four members of the commander's escort – Lieutenant Henry Lysons of the 90th, together with a corporal and two privates of the same regiment – led the way with Captain Campbell, the chief officer of the staff.

Diving into a cave from which much of the firing had been directed, they cleared it of Zulus. They returned carrying Campbell. He had been killed by a shot in the temple. Shocked by the loss of his two companions, Wood retired to the foot of the hill to bury them.

By 9 am, Buller was taking stock on the summit. His levies had rounded up a good herd of cattle and were driving them west towards Russell's force. There was a fair number of Zulus on the plateau, but they were treating Buller's troops with respect and holding their distance. There looked like being no great difficulty in converging with Russell, then driving their capture back to Kambula via the lower western plateau and Zunguin Nek. All was going to plan until Buller reached the step between the upper level, across which he had travelled, and the lower level where he should meet the western force. The plateau had narrowed to a rocky, eroding defile. Buller reined back from the ledge in astonishment. Instead of a graded descent to the lower plateau, he was looking at a drop of at least 150 feet, so sheer that, while footmen might scramble down precariously, no rider in his right mind would tackle it. He would have to turn back and take his chances on the track he had come up.

So far, he had seen no sign of the Border Horse. Assuming them to have been delayed on the ascent, he despatched his second-in-command, Captain Geoffrey Barton, Coldstream Guards, to tell Weatherley there was no point in continuing, but that he should return to Kambula by the route to the south of the mountain – in fact, exactly what Weatherley had been doing on his own initiative until he had met Wood. On his way across the plateau, Barton was to pick up a troop of the Frontier Horse which had been left to cover Buller's rear, and take it with him.

Barton had scarcely departed, when Buller had a second and greater shock. Looking to the south-east, he saw what at first appeared to him as a huge grey-speckled serpent coiling across the plain in the morning haze. Then he saw another; and three more. When the speckles resolved into white shields and black skins, he realised he was watching five columns of warriors: a Zulu impi fully 20,000 strong. Buller estimated it to be several miles distant, heading straight for Kambula on a path parallel with the southern face of Hlobane. As he collected his startled thoughts, the nearest column began to diverge from the main force and fork towards the mountain.

Cetshwayo, alarmed by the defections among the northern clans, by the British plundering and the mounting anarchy in the territory, had at last marshalled his army against Wood. Wood spotted the impi from the plain beneath the south face of Hlobane, where he had buried Lloyd and Campbell. The peril of the situation was instantly obvious. Not only were his men on Hlobane directly threatened by the approaching right wing of the enemy – if they did not get away before the main Zulu army drew abreast the west end of the mountain, retreat to Kambula would be impossible. Wood wrote a brief message for Russell and sent Lysons racing west with it. The message warned of the approaching enemy and told Russell to leave the plateau and get down to Zunguin Nek.

Russell had needed no warning. Like Buller, he had sighted the impi before Wood. Like Buller, too, he had discovered the impossibility of joining forces across the fearsome step. Convinced he could not help the force on the higher plateau, Russell began to evacuate Hlobane at all speed, driving his captured cattle before him. He had reached the foot of the western declivity when Lysons arrived with the message to get to Zunguin Nek. In point of fact, he was already there, on the ground between Hlobane and Zunguin. Russell, however, took the nek to mean the gap between the far end of Zunguin and a further range to the north-west. It made sense. Russell's nek was six miles in a direct line of retirement from the Zulu advance, it placed the heights between himself and the impi, and it could be regarded as a detour route to Kambula. Without further delay, he marched his force away from the action.

Buller's first thought on sighting the impi was for Weatherley. He had just despatched Barton with orders that would place the Border Horse in the open against the south face of Hlobane – practically in the path of 20,000 Zulus. Bawling to two of his horsemen, he sent them galloping after Barton to amend the message. The Border Horse, he now instructed, should retire 'to the right' of the mountain. Since they would be retiring west, this would mean turning left at the end of the descent, skirting the eastern tip of Hlobane and making for Kambula along the north side of the mountain, thus screened from the impi. Unfortunately, the phrasing of the order was ambiguous. Barton, taking it to mean a right turn at the foot of the cliff, assumed that this second order was a confirmation of the first.

Reaching Weatherley near the bottom of the trail, Barton relayed the instructions as he saw them. The Border Horse, now joined by Barton's troop of Frontier Horse, duly turned right along the south face and immediately found themselves trapped by the main body of the impi, whose van was already in advance of them, and whose flank faced them across the plain to the south. The only course was to turn for the eastern tip, as Buller had intended, and escape to the north. But they were too late. The detached right wing of the impi had already cut in behind them. There were sixty Border Horse, twenty Frontier Horse, and the officers. Spurring their mounts, they charged for the eastern tip in a desperate bid to break out north.

The Zulu right horn faced them unflinchingly, and the charge was smothered by stabbing warriors. Ten riders broke through.

Archibald Forbes, the war correspondent.
Sketch by Frederic Villiers.
The National Portrait Gallery, London

Above right Colonel Sir Evelyn Wood,
V.C., K.C.B.
The National Army Museum

Right A Swazi warrior with
Colonel Wood's irregular forces.
From Crealock's sketchbook.
*The Regimental Museum of the
Sherwood Foresters*

One of Wood's Irregulars
a Swazi

Colonel Charles Knight Pearson.
The Butts Regimental Museum

Above Sir Henry Bartle Frere. Painting by G. Reid.
The National Portrait Gallery, London
Above right Sir Henry Bulwer. From Crealock's
sketchbook.
The Regimental Museum of the Sherwood Foresters
Below The 13th Light Infantry at Ulundi. Painting
by Orlando Norie

Top The mouth of the River Tugela, with British
supplies in the foreground.
The National Army Museum

Above A typical Boer group pictured shortly after
the Zulu War.
The National Army Museum

Top The death mask of Prince Louis Napoleon.
From Crealock's sketchbook, inscribed: 'June 1st
1879, Zululand, he bore 18 wounds in his front.'
The Regimental Museum of the Sherwood Foresters

Above The capture of King Cetshwayo. Pictured
by Major Marten, King's Dragoon Guards,
depicted with drawn sword.
The National Army Museum

Top left King Cetshwayo's head-dress, now in the National Army Museum. *The National Army Museum*

Top right King Cetshwayo's sceptre and shield and a Zulu assegai (blade bent) found beside the body of Prince Louis Napoleon. *The Nottingham Castle Museum*

Above left King Cetshwayo, 'uncivilised', circa 1880. *The Radio Times Hulton Picture Library*

Above right King Cetshwayo, 'civilised', in exile. *The Radio Times Hulton Picture Library*

A Mite More Terror

The rest, including Barton, Weatherley and Weatherley's son, were massacred. The soldier author of *The Zulu Campaign* provided an illuminating Victorian vignette of the boy and his father in their agony:

When all save honour seemed lost [wrote Major Ashe], Weatherley placed his beloved boy upon his best horse and, kissing him on the forehead, commended him to another Father's care, and implored him to overtake the nearest group of the British horse, which seemed at that time to be cutting its way out. The boy clung to his father and begged to be allowed to stay by his side and share his life or death. The contrast was characteristic – the man, a bearded, bronzed and hardy *sabreur*, with a father's tears upon his cheek, while the blue-eyed and fair-haired lad, with much of the beauty of a girl in his appearance, was calmly and with a smile of delight loading his father's favourite carbine. When the two noble hearts were last seen, the father, wounded to death with cruel assegais, was clasping the boy's hand with his left, while his right cut down the brawny savages who came to despoil him of his charge.

On the plateau, Buller's situation had begun to seem desperate. Retreat to the east was impossible. The Zulus on the height, encouraged by the huge reinforcements below, were pressing boldly, squeezing him into the defile above the step. Here, all semblance of a rearguard action had broken down. Men, horses and bellowing cattle were swirling towards the sudden drop to the lower table, then shying back from the crumbling brink.

Buller and his officers shouted them forward. The 150-foot plunge was now their only hope, and unless they could get their mounts down with them they were still finished, for the possibility of crossing the plain below on foot was increasingly improbable. The Zulu impi was fast approaching Zunguin Nek. In ones and twos at first, then in a chaotic avalanche, the troopers urged their terrified animals over the brink and went sliding and sprawling down the rocky slope. Zulu snipers picked off the hesitant horses at the top; others broke their necks, or limbs, as they crashed down. One trooper stood gawping at the perilous drop, then shot himself.

Buller thundered back up the defile on a huge sandy charger, blazing at Zulus with his pistol, urging the stragglers along, assisting the horseless and wounded. Piet Uys, with one of the two sons in his party, was hovering in the rocks, firing whenever the warriors came too close. Buller saw Captain D'Arcy, one of his cavalry officers, retiring on foot. D'Arcy had mounted a wounded trooper on his own animal and sent him forward. Heaving the captain up behind him, Buller took him to the step, then plunged back, cussing, into the fight to rescue two more men. Lieutenant Everitt had had his horse killed under him. Buller carried him ahead, then returned for Trooper Rundell, whose mount had collapsed from exhaustion.

The Zulu skirmishers were eighty yards away when Buller dragged Rundell on to the quarters of his charger and careered down the defile. They were among the last to negotiate the torn and now bloody slope. Uys, spotting his second son struggling to drag two horses from the path of the oncoming enemy, started back to help him. A Zulu leaped on the Boer's small grey pony and planted a spear between the old man's shoulder-blades.

The foot of the step was now thick with equine carcasses, and the tattered force was streaming across the lower plateau, dropping to the plain below. Buller's levies had been the first to reach Zunguin Nek, negotiating the slopes unencumbered by equipment and frightened animals. On the flat, however, their advantage dissolved with tragic alacrity. Few escaped the spears of the swarming impi. The surviving horses now saved Buller's troopers from the same fate. Two to a mount, they flailed the weary beasts forward with spurred heels, fleeing in ragged groups for Kambula. Buller reached the camp on a drained animal, immediately saddled a fresh one, and spent half the night scouring the plain for survivors.

Wood, who had taken refuge on Zunguin hill after searching in vain for Russell's force, had witnessed the rout helplessly, watched the Zulu army camp down on Zunguin Nek, then returned to count his losses. Almost a hundred Europeans had been killed, including fifteen officers, and many more were either wounded or missing. At least twice as many Natal levies had lost their lives, and both Russell's levies and Uhamu's men had decamped. A substantial portion of the cavalry was now without horses. Five VCs were to be awarded as a result of the ill-fated action, among their recipients Buller, Lysons and a Private Fowler, the last two cited for their charge on the cave where Campbell had been killed. But Hlobane, like Intombe, made scant impact on the outer world, where they deemed mistakes best forgotten. Nor was there time at Kambula to recriminate. The camp could expect to be attacked as soon as the impi stirred from its night at Zunguin Nek.

Chapter Nine

KAMBULA
AND
GINGINDHLOVU

ᘒᏰ᎓ᎍᕒ

And that it was great pity, so it was,
This villainous saltpetre should be digg'd
Out of the bowels of the harmless earth,
Which many a good tall fellow had destroy'd.

Shakespeare,
King Henry IV

CHARLES PEARSON was one of those men, familiar to late nine-teenth-century Britain, who believed that if a job was worth doing it was worth doing substantially. Already, he had left behind him the sturdiest defences of the campaign in Forts Pearson and Tenedos, and when his officers elected to stay at Eshowe he set about building a regular stronghold. Basically, it was a rectangular enclosure, though somewhat widening at one end, where the far wall formed a point, giving the overall plan roughly the outline of a firework rocket. The main entrance was at the narrower end – approximately, by the same analogy, where the touch-paper would be sited. Inside, the three stone buildings of the mission were supplemented by a number of storage and guard huts.

The fortifications were formidable. Beyond the outer wall, itself six feet high and set with loopholes and gun emplacements, was a deep ditch twelve feet wide and studded at the bottom with sharpened stakes. Farther afield, the approaches were mined with dynamite. According to a description relayed to the *Cape Argus*:

> two well-built curtain walls ran out from the southern angles, enclosing a fine kraal for cattle and horses; and at its end was constructed an irregular redoubt, with a deep ditch and thick mud walls, defended by gigantic spiky thorns laid along the parapet. Day by day, the troops, when not on other duty, were employed in felling trees to form *abattis*, hewing out gabions, cutting loopholes, filling sandbags and contriving every species of entanglement.

Some of the defences were so massive, proclaimed the same source, that they were proof against field artillery, let alone the spears and muskets of the Zulus.

> Each face of the fort was cleared up to 800 yards, shelter trenches were dug for the first line of defence, and the ranges were carefully marked for artillery and rifle fire. Every man had his proper place assigned to him, and was in it on three minutes' notice.

The Buffs were allocated the long north wall and the short side with the main gate, the Lanarkshire men were detailed to the south wall, while the naval brigade and engineers held the pointed east face. Cannon, rocket tubes and Gatling poked their muzzles from barricades which might have repulsed the entire forces of Africa.

Since none of those forces contemplated attacking the fortress – the Zulus merely maintained a discreet watch – siege life at Eshowe was rather less than arduous. The bands of the Buffs and Lanarkshire gave concerts. The oxen in the kraal were turned out to graze in the morning and herded back in leisurely fashion before dusk. Officers and mounted patrols rode widely through the surrounding terrain without attracting hostility. Heliograph communication was established with the Tugela, by which Pearson learned, among other things, that his wife had given birth to a daughter. Like more celebrated sieges of the era, the immediate dangers were grossly inflated by popular imagination. The real problems were long term. Food supplies would be adequate until April. Lack of bedding, coupled with the damp nights, could be expected to take a toll in sickness. Medicaments were not plentiful.

By the end of February, the sick bay established in the mission church was crowded. Twenty-five men were down, mostly with fever or dysentery, and two patients, the captain of the Buffs and the boy Coker who had commanded the Gatling crew, had died. Chelmsford had visited Fort Pearson earlier in the month to consider the possibility of relieving Eshowe, but had decided his resources were inadequate. Efforts to raise fresh volunteers from Natal to rebuild his smashed force had not met with great success. His record did not inspire confidence, and the settlers who remained on their holdings had work to do. Governor Bulwer, having opposed the war from the outset, was unco-operative over supplies and recruitment, more concerned to save the colony's already over strained economy from collapse.

At the beginning of March, Chelmsford again contemplated a relief mission. On the 5th of that month, Pearson received a heliographed message from a Colonel Drury Lowe, RA, on the Tugela:

> About 13th instant, by general's orders, I advance to support you with 1,000 men, besides natives, as far as Inyezane. Be prepared to sally out to meet me with your surplus garrison ... Make answer by flag on church.

Pearson ordered a flag to be run up, but since this was not acknowledged, and the sky was now overcast, he improvised a fire balloon made of tracing paper; also a screen, 15 feet by 12 feet, set on the skyline. When both devices failed, a messenger was despatched with orders to circuit the intervening countryside, which was thick with scouting Zulus, and tell Lowe the garrison would be ready on the appointed day. With much enthusiasm, Pearson's men began to clear a path through an adjacent wood in order to get guns and wagons out more rapidly than by the existing track. The next word from Lowe was disappointing. The relief had been postponed until 1 April.

By mid-March, the garrison had consumed all its slaughter beasts and was reduced to eating draft oxen. To replenish his stock of meat, and raise camp morale, Pearson resolved to rustle cattle from Dabulamanzi's kraal, near Gingindhlovu. A hundred bayonets from the Buffs and Lanarkshire, twenty-five naval men with the Gatling and a body of mounted scouts set out on this audacious mission. They reached a steep kloof in some hills near the kraal after an apprehensive night on the veld, brushed off a splutter of musket fire, and charged through the huts, burning, destroying, stampeding women, children and cattle. Enthusiasm for the task waned when Dabulamanzi's men rallied and moved to surround the raiders. Abandoning their loot, the British raced for safety, pursued by a growing host of infuriated warriors.

The cumbersome Gatling, so effective in the right conditions, was an unwanted impediment in a swift retreat over rough ground and flooded spruits, and the Zulus gained steadily on the ravishers of their homes. With evening at hand, and perhaps an hour's march before them, the raiders encountered a low mist which screened them from the enemy. They were now in forest immediately below Eshowe, struggling uphill towards the fort. Suddenly, dark objects were spotted through the murk to the left. According to one report:

> so fitful was the view, that the men were unable to ascertain whether they were Zulus or some of the larger species of baboon ... before many minutes, however, they could plainly see that a large body of the enemy had, by the most tremendous pedestrian feat, succeeded in getting almost on a level with them, in a position to assail them in flank.

Pearson's marauders narrowly regained the cover of Eshowe thanks largely to ten mounted scouts who, galloping to high ground some 500 yards from the Zulus, delayed them with a spasm of rapid and well-directed fire. By the time the last man reached safety in the fort, the sun had disappeared completely. After all efforts, the party had not captured a single head of cattle, returning empty-handed save for two paltry bags of mealies. A second expedition, smaller and unencumbered by the Gatling, did manage to seize thirty-five fat beasts grazing on the flats of the Inyezane. The achievement was greeted by great excitement in the camp. A dwindling diet had added to the sick roll. A hundred men a day were now reporting for treatment, apart from those in hospital, and more than twenty had died.

On 20 March, Pearson heard from the Tugela that the column to relieve him would set out on the 29th. He was to hold 500 men in readiness to assist over the last few miles, if necessary. The closing nights of the month saw everyone at Eshowe seeking a view of the plains below, where the distant twinkle of fires in the column's bivouacks drew a stage nearer with each dusk.

On 1 April, Pearson's officers, sweeping the Inyezane valley with their glasses, saw the first miniature image of horsemen – Chelmsford's scouts – then the coil of marching troops and wagons, approaching the bamboo and hippopotami-fringed river. Night fell with the column in laager, and few at Eshowe inclined to sleep. Four hours' march would bring relief to the stranded garrison. At dawn, Pearson trained his glasses on the plain to watch the column break camp. He saw a very different activity. The wagons were still in laager. Suddenly, white puffs of powder smoke erupted from the British lines. Artillery rumbled. The black tide everyone recognised broke from cover and surged inward from three sides.

The first of Chelmsford's overseas reinforcements – a company of Connaught Rangers and an artillery battalion from St Helena – had arrived at Durban on HMS *Shah* on 6 March. Between them, the *Shah* and another vessel, HMS *Boadicea*, landed upward of 600 men from their own complements to swell the Naval Brigade. By the twentieth, the 57th Regiment, the West Middlesex, had followed at battalion strength, plus the 91st, the Argyllshire Highlanders, also at battalion strength, and six companies of light infantry from the 60th Foot, the King's Royal Rifle Corps. At this stage, the general felt sufficiently confident to commit himself to a bid for Eshowe at the end of the month, especially if Wood could contrive a northerly diversion. Had he known, he need not have worried on the last point, for Cetshwayo's premier, Mnyamana, together with the ageing victor of Isandhlwana,

Tshingwayo, and eight regiments re-mustered from the Ulundi area, were already heading north when Wood projected the Hlobane excursion.

On the morning of the 29th, as Chelmsford's relief column left the Tugela for Eshowe, Tshingwayo marched from Zunguin's Nek for Kambula, now joined by the abaQulusi. The Zulu scouts found Wood in a strong position. His camp, at the eastern end of a long east-to-west ridge, was made up of three components: firstly, a stone-walled redoubt on an eminence near the head of the ridge; secondly, the main laager sprawled across the neck of the ridge on the west side of the redoubt; and thirdly, a smaller cattle laager between these two and somewhat to the south, where the side of the ridge fell away in a steep cliff. The wagons forming the two laagers had been pulled up close and chained together. Tshingwayo, drawing in sight a short while before noon, held his impi off to the south and took a good look. It was not inviting, but he knew Wood's losses had been serious the day before, and that he might expect to find the garrison in poor order.

It was certainly depleted. Apart from those who would never return from Hlobane, and the wounded now quartered within the main laager, Wood had been deserted by most of his surviving levies, by the remainder of Uhamu's men, and by his Boer horsemen who, with Piet Uys dead, had decamped that very morning. He had, however, the best part of his two line battalions intact, and his artillery. The latter was deployed in the open spaces between the laagers and the redoubt; the infantry largely in the main laager, with a company of Somersetshire in the cattle laager and a company each of Somersetshire and Perthshire in the redoubt with Wood himself.

If Tshingwayo thought he had a chance against such odds, he was sadly deluded. Rorke's Drift had shown that modern infantry behind cover could beat off the most resolute spearmen, though outnumbered forty to one. At Kambula, the ratio was more like ten to one, the position was better prepared than at Rorke's Drift, and the defenders had rockets and field guns. It was a contest only so far as the Zulus were determined on self-sacrifice.

In fact, though the action was relatively extended, lasting more than four hours, it was protracted more by the shelter afforded the attackers by dead ground on the slopes of the ridge than by any enduring hope of success in the Zulu ranks.

Having extended his army along the south of the camp, out of gun range, Tshingwayo pushed forward the traditional embracing horns and drew the breast of the impi towards the steep south face of the ridge. Seeing that the right horn was some way in advance of the left, Buller suggested he should take a party of Frontier Horse towards it and try to lure the warriors into a premature attack. The idea of beating the enemy in detail appealed to Wood, who gave his permission. Advancing into range of the right horn, Buller's men dismounted, pumped a provocative volley into the Zulus, re-mounted and started back for their own lines.

The scheme worked almost too perfectly. Almost as a man, the loping column sprang forward, stung from its customary discipline, and raced 'at a tremendous pace' after the horsemen. What Buller had planned as an orderly retirement became a breakneck flight for the laager. One trooper, unable to re-mount his frightened horse, was narrowly rescued by an officer.

As the troops regained safety, the artillery smashed into the charging warriors who veered right, paused shortly while their breathless indunas called up reserves, then hurled themselves at the north ridge. From the facing wagons of the main laager, the Perthshires watched them top the rise in thousands – umCijo, umBonambi, umHlanga and uNokenke – and blazed at a blanket target. So appalling were the Zulu losses that for all their reckless courage, according to the soldier author of *With the Irregulars in the Transvaal and Zululand*, they never seriously troubled the north face again. A handful reached the wagons and were thrown back at bayonet point. The rest streamed away, supporting their casualties, hammered by case from the field guns. Two warriors, carrying a wounded chief, staggered across the front of the redoubt and were dropped by the rifles there.

The action now devolved chiefly on the cattle kraal by the south cliff. Huddling under the lip, then bursting forward in large numbers, the warriors swarmed among the restive animals until the company of Somersetshire there was quickly fighting a retiring action to the redoubt. With a base on the ridge, the Zulus clambered up the cliff in a dense mass. From the cover of the cattle laager they could storm either of the other stockades, or charge the artillery, and Wood sent a message to Major Robert Hackett, in the main laager, to advance with two companies of Perthshire and drive the Zulus in the south back over the cliff.

Hackett emerged in front of the artillery, formed line and started his men forward steadily, firing as they advanced. The left of the line was approaching the north face of the cattle laager; the right, pushing into the space between the laagers to repulse the Zulus gathering at the lip of the ridge there.

Bob Hackett was an old-type regimental officer. After nearly a quarter of a century's service, he expected no further promotion, nor particularly wanted it. The future in any army which now required officers to pass exams like schoolboys lay, he might have thought, with lads such as Arthur Bright, a twenty-one-year-old subaltern who now advanced with him. Smart, articulate, a good musician and a talented artist, Bright was hardly the type who would have joined the service before Cardwell's day. He typified the new image inspired by Wolseley and the modern brigade. With Hackett and Bright was Colour Sergeant McAllen, already wounded but patched up and ready for more punishment.

Hackett's men, gaining the wall of the cattle laager, poured a crippling fire on the warriors clustered inside, while the right of the line opened destructively on those scrambling up the slope. 'Dark bodies with painted shields strewed all the ground,' a contemporary report had it, 'or rolled down the rocks with bloody and gaping wounds.' But the Zulus continued to climb in such numbers, and with such suicidal fearlessness, that Hackett, now under an aggravating barrage from enemy snipers, had his bugler signal a withdrawal to the main laager. Bright saw McAllen killed by a bullet, then went down with one through his own thigh. He was dragged to cover not badly wounded, but bled to death after incompetent medical treatment. Hackett felt a searing blow on his temple and lost his vision. Though his life was saved, he did not regain his sight.

Wood now contented himself with pinning the enemy in the cattle laager by fire from the other posts. This was contrived to such effect that the Zulus could neither remove the animals to the rear nor reach the main laager to the front. Time and again, they charged across the open ground, to be decimated by the rifles of the Perthshire holding the south face. Meanwhile, the artillery, performing a kind of cumbersome ballet between the laager and the redoubt, manoeuvred to blast the Zulu regiments from their assembly points. By mid-afternoon, Tshingwayo's men were more concerned with protecting themselves from the shellfire, and from Wood's cavalry which was beginning to sally against their shelters, than with any remaining hope of a victory.

At about 5.30, the impi began to extricate itself. Mustering as many men as could be mounted, Buller and Russell harried the retiring regiments for some miles, until the hills and encroaching dusk obscured them. Closer to camp, companies of infantry scoured the battleground and surrounding slopes killing many Zulu wounded and other stragglers found in concealment. According to the War Office report, 1,500 Zulu bodies were counted before nightfall, though many were recovered by comrades who returned under cover of darkness. An estimated 2,000 had died as a result of the attack, and at least as many had been injured. By contrast, the British losses were 29 dead or dying, and 55 more wounded. Yesterday, Wood had failed ignominiously in his quest for victory. Today, the enemy had presented it to him on a plate.

Chelmsford did not know it, but when the vanguard of his relief column camped inside Zululand on the evening of the 29th, he had become the beneficiary of a diversion on a scale he had not dared to contemplate. The bulk of Cetshwayo's armed force had marched against Kambula and was now hungry, crippled and disorganised in the north. Less than half as many warriors remained to contest the passage to Pearson's fort.

These, though operating in the area of Dabulamanzi's land,

had been placed by Cetshwayo under a fresh general, a chief named Somopo. The king wanted no more of his younger brother's adventures. His aim was still to neutralise the right wing of the invasion with the minimum of violence, and to this end Somopo's brief was to prevent the relief at as light a cost to his regiments as possible. One possibility would be to ambush the two-mile-long column at a river crossing and destroy the supply wagons. This was what Umatyiya had been attempting against Pearson at Inyezane when the trap had been sprung prematurely by the levies. Another would be to strand the supplies by raiding the expedition's draft oxen at a grazing halt.

Unfortunately for Somopo, the relief column did not follow Pearson's route but took an easterly detour, hugging the coast for the first half of its journey. The coastal flats, as Chelmsford wisely reasoned, were notably lacking in the type of cover required to mount an ambush or a surprise raid. By the time the snaking train of troops and wagons struck inland on the morning of 1 April, time was running short for the Zulu chief. One more stop – one more river, the Inyezane – and the column would be at Eshowe the next day. The scope for refinements was limited. Somopo decided to attack at dawn on 2 April, advancing under cover of the morning mist.

Chelmsford, personally commanding the relief force, was not repeating the mistakes of his earlier incursion. This time, there were no open camps. At every nightfall, the general had laagered and entrenched, and his position on the evening of 1 April was a particularly good one. About six miles downstream from Pearson's crossing of the Inyezane, beside the ravaged kraal of Gingindhlovu, was a grassy eminence in a broad V of ground formed by the intersection of the Inyezane with a tributary, the Gingindhlovu stream. Tall, feathery grass quilted the low land, giving on to swampy flats by the river banks, where wild animals watered at dawn and dusk. Chelmsford placed his 160-odd wagons and carts in a square laager atop the rise, surrounding it with a trench and abattis.

Before turning in, the units were allocated their stations, the cavalry, staff and ammunition within the wagon wall, the infantry outside it, behind the trench and waist-high rampart. On the leading station, facing north-west to the Inyezane and the continuing path to Eshowe, were the companies of the 60th Rifles (conspicuous for the dark green tunics the regiment wore against the normal red of the British line), supported at the angles by blue-jackets from the HMS *Shah* and the HMS *Tenedos* with Gatling guns. On the right face was the West Middlesex, and on the rear the Argyllshire Highlanders. Of the two rear angles, the right incorporated a couple of Royal Artillery 7-pounders; the left, another Gatling and a rocket battery. The remaining left face was covered by two more companies of the Highlanders, three of the Buffs and five of the Lanarkshire.

Though many of the troops were unseasoned, this was the strongest British force yet to enter Zululand – well over 4,000 of horse and infantry, of whom less than a quarter were Africans. Bristling with cannon, rockets and *mitrailleuse*, the camp was a ludicrous target for Somopo, whose spearmen numbered at most 12,000.

Nevertheless, as dawn broke on the 2nd, his regiments padded towards Gingindhlovu through the mist which presaged the rising sun. Chelmsford's pickets, glimpsing the haze-shrouded impi, raced back to the laager to raise the warning. The main Zulu force was approaching from due north, across flat ground, with the Inyezane to its left and some high land known as Umisi hill on its right. Hopefully, Somopo had entrusted his warriors to the flimsy cover of the tall grass. His flanking forces – the right sweeping across Umisi hill to strike west; the left fording the river to cut back south-east – were no better off. Whichever way they came, there was no shelter on the long slopes.

It could result only in wholesale suicide.

Behind the compact lines of British infantry, civilian drivers and other veteran colonials sat in the wagons with long-barrelled *roers*, the guns they used on big game, swigging liquor and smacking their lips in anticipation. Chelmsford was still wearing a woollen nightcap to keep his ears warm.

Suddenly, the mist dissolved and the warriors were in full sight, less than a mile away. 'Their white and coloured shields, the crests of leopard skin and feathers, the wild ox-tails dangling from their necks, gave them an unearthly appearance,' wrote one witness. 'Every ten or fifteen yards, their line would halt ... then rush on with a sort of measured dance, while a humming or buzzing sound in time to their movements was kept up.'

At a thousand yards, a Gatling opened the slaughter with a short burst. The black mass ducked into the grass, to reappear closer. Rockets and shells tore terrible gaps in the regiments. Still the Zulus came on. At 300 yards, the infantry fired its first volley. A wall of flame spread along the laager as rifle and Gatling zoned the target at callous range. Somopo's men reeled and wavered. No troops in the world could have been expected to stand unprotected in such fire. Yet for almost half an hour, groups of warriors hurled themselves to within twenty yards of the trenches, to be smashed into the torn grass where hundreds of their compatriots lay dead or in agony.

When the tortured impi finally abandoned its cruel task, a thousand dead were strewn around the laager, or where Chelmsford's cavalry and levies pitched into the line of retreat across the Inyezane. The British had lost thirteen men, killed by stray shots from those Zulus who possessed firearms. A single warrior had penetrated the defences − a mere boy, he had continued charging when his comrades were wiped out, had leaped the trench and rampart and been captured unharmed. He was adopted by the seamen of the HMS *Boadicea* as a mascot.

Pearson's sally from Eshowe to support the relief force had not materialised. It would have taken his men four hours to reach Gingindhlovu. The action was over in less than half that time. Next day, having spent the rest of the 2nd at the laager, Chelmsford advanced to Eshowe with the Middlesex, the 60th, the Argyllshire and part of the supply train. For much of the way, the trail was littered with trappings and weapons abandoned by the disillusioned regiments of Somopo, among them a number of rifles and swords once possessed by officers and men of the 24th. Before the final uphill slog to the fort, the troops were issued with special rations of rum, and the Highlanders went forward with all their pipes playing. The beleaguered garrison welcomed them with wild cheers and a stampede of congratulation which swept aside all discipline.

Chelmsford wasted little time at Eshowe. On 4 April, he despatched his mounted troops in a bid to catch Dabulamanzi, who reportedly was recuperating from the battle at a kraal a few miles away. John Dunn, the adventurer who had insinuated himself into Cetshwayo's confidence and enjoyed generous grants of land and privilege from the king, rode on the mission. Dunn had quickly proved the nature of his friendship when it became evident that the British invasion threat was serious. With no doubt as to the inevitability of the outcome, he had hastened to place his special knowledge of the country at Chelmsford's service – an act for which, as he surmised, he would duly be rewarded. Now, he took a gun with him to hunt his former friend and neighbour, the brother of the king who had trusted him.

Dabulamanzi was not to be caught so easily. The British riders, advancing at a canter to surround the kraal, found it deserted. With customary thoroughness, they had begun to burn the dwellings when a shot rang out from a height at long range. Raising his glasses, Dunn recognised the Zulu captain and fired back. After a profitless duel, the protagonists went their respective ways.

On 5 April, having destroyed as much of the fort at Eshowe as time would permit, Chelmsford started back to Gingindhlovu in the rear of Pearson, who had gone ahead some hours earlier. The spruits were swollen and the journey, a slow one, was distinguished by a painful accident. Dunn, returning to camp after dark on the 6th with a scouting party, ran into a jittery sentry. The sentry fired without challenging. The scouts, retiring for cover, were now spotted by a picket of the 60th, who joined the fire on them. In the confusion which ensued, four men were killed and about a dozen wounded. Chelmsford reached Gingindhlovu the next day, left Colonel Wykeham Pemberton of the 60th in charge, and rode straight on with his own staff to the Tugela and Natal.

Nearly three months after the start of his invasion, more than the time originally allowed for its completion and the subjugation of Zululand, the general had been forced out of the kingdom with what remained of one column, had virtually withdrawn a second, while the third was still camped on the northern borderlands, just about where it had kicked off. By an extraordinary display of individual courage and national dedication, an insular, pastoral people still fighting with shields and spears had driven off a modern European aggressor whose forces had learned their job across half the world. It had cost the Zulus mortal wounds. At a conservative estimate, 7,000 warriors had been killed and as many badly injured. Perhaps one in every two men of Cetshwayo's army had felt a British bullet. Worse, Kambula and Gingindhlovu had at last revealed the pathetic futility of such sacrifice.

The hunters might have retired before the lion's charge, but the lion lay mangled and bleeding from their gunshots. They would be back to deliver the *coup de grâce*.

Chapter Ten

ULUNDI

Just send in your Chief an' surrender – it's
worse if you fights or you runs:
You can go where you please, you can skid up
the trees, but you can't get away from the guns!

> Rudyard Kipling,
> 'Screw-guns'

CURIOUSLY, the final stage of the British campaign to exterminate Zulu resistance was overshadowed by two personalities who took little part in it. The more significant of these, since he fashioned the aftermath, was Sir Garnet Wolseley. Though the home government had refused to be coerced by public outcry at the time of Isandhlwana into action against Frere or Chelmsford, it was not long after the furore had abated when steps were taken to diminish their authority in South Africa. Naturally, there was no intention of slighting the gentlemen, explained the Queen's ministers, but 'the arrangement under which the chief military and civil authority in the neighbourhood of the seat of war was distributed between four persons – Sir Bartle Frere, Sir Henry Bulwer, Lord Chelmsford and Colonel Lanyon (Lieutenant Governor of the Transvaal) – could no longer be deemed adequate'. Accordingly, Her Majesty's Government had appointed General Wolseley High Commissioner, with overall command in the area. However delicately it might be put to them, Wolseley's appointment was less than a compliment to Chelmsford and his staff. They had taken the blows of the war and had no wish to see someone else step in and cream the glory at the finish. Chelmsford meant to have his victory. After that, he would be ready to bow out. In the second week of April, he returned to Durban from the Lower Drift and, on the 12th, inspected reinforcements which had arrived since his departure for Eshowe.

They were impressive. Among the units, which had disembarked from a fleet including some of the latest steam vessels in service, were two crack cavalry regiments, the 1st Dragoon Guards and the 17th Lancers; three new infantry regiments, the 21st Foot, Royal Scots Fusiliers, the 58th Foot, Rutlandshire Regiment, and the 94th Foot Connaught Rangers; and drafts for most of the other corps in the Cape colony, among them two batteries of artillery and a fresh contingent of engineers. In all, there were more than 400 new officers, about 10,000 other ranks and 1,870 horses. With his existing troops, this gave Chelmsford something like 16,000 Europeans and 7,000 levies – a force that could have vanquished many times the residue of Cetshwayo's stricken army.

With the reinforcements from England came the second of the celebrities destined to haunt Chelmsford's overwhelming descent on Ulundi. Prince Louis Napoleon, son of the Empress Eugénie by the late Napoleon III of France, had joined the Royal Military Academy at Woolwich in 1872 and graduated three years later with some distinction, being top of his class in fencing and riding. Having passed as a soldier, Louis had killed time on the social rounds of Europe awaiting the day, craved by his mother and their monarchist supporters, when the republic would falter and a Napoleon would rise again at the head of France. At the time of Isandhlwana, Louis was twenty-two, the republic still intact, the life of a jobless royal celebrity palling. Back in England, among the officer friends with whom he felt most at ease, he hit on the idea of volunteering for service in Zululand.

The notion had several attractions. It was manly and adventurous, campaign experience would boost his credibility as a military leader, it would cement his good relationship with England, and there could be no diplomatic drawbacks to fighting

African savages. Disraeli had thought otherwise. To the annoyance of Eugénie and Queen Victoria, who considered the plan admirable, he flatly refused to let Louis join the British ranks in Zululand. It was left to the Duke of Cambridge to strike an acceptable compromise.

Louis should go as a privileged spectator – 'to see as much as he can with the columns in the field'. Whatever Chelmsford's misgivings, he could only co-operate.

> He is a fine young fellow [Cambridge wrote of the prince], full of spirit and pluck, having many old cadet friends ... he will undoubtedly find no difficulty in getting on and if you can help him in any other way please do so. My only anxiety on his conduct would be that he is too *plucky* and *go ahead*.

'Go ahead' proved an apt phrase. By the end of May, Chelmsford had sorted out his logistical problems, done a good deal of scouting and was consolidated in north and south Zululand ready for the strike at Ulundi. His invasion force was now in two divisions. The 1st division, under General Henry Hope Crealock, a veteran of the Crimea, India, China and Canada, was based on Durban and stretched through Fort Pearson along the coastal road to the Inyezane. It comprised, among others, the 3rd, 57th, 60th, 88th, 91st and 99th Regiments. The 2nd division – whose commander, General Edward Newdigate, like Glyn before him, was upstaged by Chelmsford's presence with his force – rested on Pietermaritzburg and Utrecht, advancing south towards Ulundi. The 21st, 58th and 94th were at the Blood River with the 17th Lancers, a squadron of Dragoons, twelve field guns and contingents of levies and irregulars. Wood, whose force now constituted a flying column with the division, had already crossed the river. To the front of Wood was the ubiquitous Buller with his horse troops. And in the van of them all, by some compound of circumstance which would have horrified Disraeli, rode his royal highness Prince Louis Napoleon.

On Sunday, 1 June, the 2nd division moved from the Blood River to a position near Itelezi hill, between the Buffalo and Ityotyosi rivers, prior to proceeding east to the latter next day.

The Ityotyosi flowed into the Umfolosi, and thus towards Ulundi. It had already been scouted and pronounced free of Zulus, and when Louis proposed riding ahead to make topographical notes of the countryside nobody stopped him. Restraining Louis's enthusiasm was a hard task. Even Buller had found it difficult to prevent the prince charging forward at the slightest hint of the enemy. Now he was given a small mounted escort and left to his own devices.

The prince's status appears to have been confused from the outset. As a spectator, he had no valid authority. As a royal person and graduate of a British military academy, the aura of command invested him naturally. Instinctively, he assumed control of the seven troopers of his escort, who, for their part, seem equally to have taken his leadership for granted. On this occasion, there was a further dubiety of protocol. Louis was accompanied by a Lieutenant Carey. Jahleel Carey, the son of a Devon clergyman, had been educated in France, and the two men got on well. Carey had asked, and received permission from, the officer in charge of reconnaissance, Quartermaster General Richard Harrison, to go along on the sketching trip. As far as Louis was concerned – and as Carey would later claim – Carey was present as the prince's companion. His superiors would claim he was in charge of the party.

At about 3 pm, the small band reached an isolated kraal by the Ityotyosi and paused to rest. Louis was riding a big, awkward grey, a powerful beast but a notorious buck-jumper. During the day, the prince had sketched, chatted to Carey and consistently issued the orders, even the routine drill commands for mounting, dismounting and tending the needs of the horses. Now the mounts were unsaddled and knee-haltered for grazing while the men brewed some coffee.

The kraal was deserted, but fresh ashes and a number of dogs around the huts suggested recent occupation. Between the kraal and the river was a crop of corn on which the horses browsed contentedly. Some 200 yards from the huts ran a dry water-course, eight feet deep and overgrown with high tambookie grass. The party had rested about forty minutes when Carey proposed its departure. Louis looked at his watch. 'Give the horses ten minutes more,' he said. At this point, a lone Zulu was sighted on a nearby hill, and the prince, changing his mind, ordered 'saddle-up'. The men dispersed to collect their mounts, slung on blankets and saddles, fixed girths and waited for the command to mount. It came almost simultaneously with a volley of gunfire from the grassy donga.

Startled, the horses threw their heads up and kicked off in all directions. About forty warriors now rose with a roar from the ditch and raced forward brandishing firearms and assegais. Most of the riders scrambled into their saddles, but with stirrups flying, and animals frightened by the screaming Zulus, could do little but hang on. One trooper, Rogers, lost his horse altogether. He was trying to load his carbine as the assailants closed on him.

Another, Abel, took a bullet in the back as his horse fled, and crashed to earth. Louis was still struggling to mount the big grey, which plunged and reared frantically. He had lost the near stirrup, and, with one hand on the reins, was trying to steady the stirrup leather with the other. A trooper named Le Tocq, who hailed from the Channel Islands, shouted to the prince in Norman French, urging him to hurry. Then Le Tocq's horse swept him off with the rest.

With the Zulus almost upon him, Louis had no option but to give his mount some head and attempt to vault aboard. The grey took the bit and surged forward at a gallop, dragging the Frenchman, who could do nothing but cling to a leather saddle holster. He was drawn a hundred yards before the strap broke, he sprawled to the ground and a metalled hoof struck his right arm. The remainder of the stampeding horses were in full flight, their riders wrestling for control. Carey, aware only of the few who were close to him, bawled to them to veer left towards the camp at Itelezi. Across his shoulder, Le Tocq caught a fleeting glimpse of Louis running from a group of Zulus. They all carried assegais. It was the last that was seen of the prince alive. He had no chance against the fleet warriors. Turning at bay in a small ravine, he fired two shots from his revolver before the spears drove into him.

By the time Carey had collected the survivors, there was no sight of the lost men. The kraal and donga were occupied by the Zulus and no dismounted white man could have lived there. One of the riders had caught the prince's horse. The conclusion was inescapable. To go back with five soldiers would be futile. Shocked beyond words, Carey swung his horse and led them at a gallop towards the camp. It was almost dusk before help could be raised, and a return to the kraal was postponed until the morning. When the fateful donga had been swept by lancers, the prince's body was found stripped save for a gold wristlet and a necklace containing his father's miniature. Abel had been killed by a bullet from a captured British carbine. Rogers, propped against a bank, eyes open and frozen in disbelief, had been butchered with assegais.

The news of the prince's death was the sensation of the Zulu War. In Britain, it received a press which diminished all earlier reports – even Isandhlwana – to insignificance. In France, hardened republicans who had never raised more than a sneer for the Pretender suddenly saw him as a French hero impelled to his death by callous Englishmen. On both sides, politicians and courtiers shed tears of discretion and sincerity. Queen Victoria sat up all night when she heard the tidings. The Empress Eugénie fell into a coma for two days.

The prince's body, roughly embalmed by the field surgeons, was given an infantry escort to Pietermaritzburg, thence to Durban, by sea to Capetown, and, finally, by HMS *Orontes* to England. At each stop, the crowds became larger, the church services grander, the weeping louder. By the time the corpse was ready to join the remains of Napoleon III at Chislehurst, Kent, it was unrecognisable. The formal identification was made by a dentist.

Meanwhile, a scapegoat being needed, Carey was the clear choice. Having gone along themselves with the prince's unofficial role of royal soldier and dashing leader, the officers of the division now held Carey responsible for the consequences – not least of which, their collective sense of guilt compounded the vehemence of their recriminations. Buller's first words to Carey on hearing of Louis's death had been: 'You ought to be shot, and I hope you will be.' It was not an isolated sentiment. From simply being stunned by the tragedy, Carey grew bitter. The fact that he had been the only officer in the party held unavoidable implications. He was not blind to them. On the night of the incident, he had written despairingly to his wife:

> Annie, what will you think of me! I was such a fool to stop in that camp. I feel it now, though at the time I did not see it ... Oh for some Christian sympathy! I feel so miserable and dejected! I know not what to do! Of course, all sorts of yarns will get into the papers, and without hearing my tale I shall be blamed, but honestly, between you and me, I can only be blamed for the camp. I tried to rally the men in the retreat and had no idea the poor Prince was (left) behind.

The words seem to admit his authority over the choice of the resting-place, but at a general court martial on 12 June he showed his hostile fellow officers a cool, uncontrite face, denying that command of the party was ever his and placing all responsibility on Louis. The court, presided over by Glyn, found him guilty of unsoldierly behaviour in the face of the enemy, sending him home under technical arrest to await sentence. It was too easy a disposal of the wider blame. Whatever Carey might think of the newspapers, they sprang to his defence, plausibly asserting that responsibility for the episode should be shared by a chain of command which rose to the Duke of Cambridge himself – perhaps beyond.

The British public agreed. When Carey's ship docked at Plymouth, he was greeted as a martyred hero. Though his eagerness to accept the role did him no great credit, and some of his observations on Louis were dishonourable, Eugénie begged Victoria that the matter might be dropped. Thus, with the two women who had helped to set the whole affair in motion now pressing to close it, the odd little fantasy had turned full circle. Theoretically, the Queen's whim could not reverse the army's verdict. In fact, it was otherwise. On a 'technical irregularity', the proceedings of the court martial were declared null and void. There was reference to defective orders, but no further charge was made. Carey was ordered to return to his duties. The world forgot the prince who had wished to play soldiers.

Kambula and Gingindhlovu convinced Cetshwayo that there was little option but to seek peace on British terms, however humiliating these might be. The problem, however, was still one of communication. The English language was a mystery at Ulundi, and interpreters with the invading forces were few and far between. The king might send court dignitaries and trusted chiefs to contact the enemy, but to Europeans these august embassies were nothing but groups of illiterate and semi-naked savages who, when they made any impression, were regarded as harbingers of trickery and deceit. At Eshowe and Lower Drift, royal envoys had been made captive. Others had been abused and sent packing. At the end of May, the king sent two messengers to Crealock with word that if the British soldiers withdrew from Zululand, he would comply with terms. In a special plea to Dunn, Cetshwayo asked why, since his former friend was familiar with events from the outset, could he not persuade the invaders of their injustice. 'It is too late now,' replied Dunn, 'I am powerless.' Crealock simply referred the envoys to Chelmsford.

In the first week of June, three royal envoys found Chelmsford camped on the Nondweni, a tributary of the Umfolosi somewhat nearer Ulundi than the Ityotyosi. Why, they asked him, were the British making war on the Zulu? Since there was no fair answer to the question, they further inquired what their king must do to end the hostilities and start negotiations. Chelmsford demanded the return of the draft oxen and field guns taken at Isandhlwana, together with the ceremonial surrender of a Zulu regiment, as a beginning. These terms were confirmed in writing, to be translated for the king by a Dutch trader named Cornelius Vijn, who was said to be in the neighbourhood of Ulundi.

As it happened, Vijn, whose English was hardly reliable, was far to the north. By the time he had been called to Ulundi, and had scribbled a rough version of the king's reply, and the messengers had returned to the British lines, it was 22 June. Chelmsford himself had advanced another twenty miles, and the officer they met promised to shoot them if they did not clear off. They turned tail for Ulundi without looking for the general. The message, that the British should stop burning Zulu homes and stealing cattle before Chelmsford's demands were met, had barely returned unopened to Cetshwayo when the 2nd division appeared on a height named Mtonjaneni, across the Umfolosi from Ulundi. Time for talking was running short. Cetshwayo could not ask a Zulu regiment to surrender, nor could he produce the field guns, which were far from Ulundi. Instead, he sent all the captured oxen he possessed, with a bonus of two prized elephant tusks, and avowed that the cannons had been sent for.

Chelmsford's answer was that he would wait one day for the surrender of a regiment, failing which he would descend on Ulundi. At the same time, he marshalled his army on the height, ready to advance to the Umfolosi in the morning. It was 29 June. The great Wolseley had arrived in Durban the day before, prepared to command the capture of the Zulu capital. Chelmsford meant to deny him the privilege.

Sir Garnet Wolseley had one problem. Set to join whichever of the two divisions would be at Ulundi first, he was frustrated by lack of information on Chelmsford's position. The 2nd division had virtually severed contact with its northern base. It might well be nearer Ulundi, as Wolseley saw it, than Crealock's 1st division – on the other hand, Wolseley knew where to join the 1st division. Crealock had now established a shore base, sentimentally named Port Durnford, beyond the Inyezane, towards the mouth of the Umhlatuze, the last major river before the Umfolosi. Wolseley could take a ship up the coast and be there in a few hours. The alternative – to ride south from Pietermaritzburg in search of an unco-operative Chelmsford – would involve days, not hours. The 'modern major general' decided: he would take the head of the 1st division, march light to Ulundi and end the war at a single stroke. All would be, as the popular phrase had it, 'Sir Garnet'.

Unfortunately for his plans, the surf was so high when he arrived at Port Durnford in HMS *Shah* that it was impossible to get ashore. Damp and seasick, Wolseley and his staff returned to Durban. On 3 July, they prepared to ride to Port Durnford.

Chelmsford had laagered strongly on the height overlooking the Umfolosi and Ulundi, and had scouted the river fords. From the bank of the broad stream, his patrols had heard the chanting of thousands of warriors in the military kraal of Nodwengu, between the river and the royal kraal. The sound, rising and falling in the still air, struck them as 'weird and solemn'. Messages between Chelmsford and Cetshwayo had petered out. On 3 July, Vijn left Ulundi and all communication ceased with the Zulu camp. On the envelope of the final missive from the royal court, the Dutchman had jotted a warning that the Ulundi army was still numerous, and Chelmsford had no doubt that it intended a last fight.

On the 2nd, the British had watched warriors of the umCijo turn back a herd of white cattle being driven towards the ford as a further peace offering from Cetshwayo. On the morning of the 3rd, a sputtering musket fire was opened on troopers watering their horses at the river.

Shortly after noon that day, Chelmsford ordered Buller to cross the Umfolosi with his mounted irregulars and scout towards Ulundi. They went off in fine style, breasting the stream in force and cantering briskly up the slope on the far bank, to disappear over a grassy ridge. Before long, there was firing and the horsemen reappeared helter-skelter, some of them doubled up. They had encountered a substantial force of Zulus and escaped, not without losses, after a hot chase. Nevertheless, Buller's report was heartening. He had penetrated beyond Nodwengu and had seen nothing that might prevent a general advance to Ulundi. Chelmsford resolved to seize the prize next day.

The division crossed the river at dawn, Buller once more in the van. Leaving the imperial troops in their rear, the irregulars spurred up the initial slopes and gazed ahead. Kraals dotted the landscape. The track to Ulundi curled between Nodwengu barracks and, on its left, a circular burial ground containing Mpande's grave, then over a smooth rise before descending to a stream named the Mbilane. On flat ground beyond the stream, in a huge fenced ring, lay the hundreds of beehive huts of Ulundi, dominated by the royal residence.

It was a deceptively tranquil scene.

Here and there, tamarind and acacia trees broke the skyline; aloe, mimosa and convolvuli grew in the scented bush; bees had begun to forage in the rising sun. Only the vultures, feeding on the carrion of yesterday's action, hinted at something more violent. For a moment, the veld seemed empty save for the flora and fauna, then a bunch of Zulus scudded over a distant ridge, followed by a larger party, and the slopes were suddenly clustered with warriors. Behind, Buller's troopers heard the strains of martial music, and, turning, encountered a mesmeric sight.

Chelmsford's army was advancing in a meticulously described hollow square, bands playing, colours flying, with the steady precision of parade-ground ceremonial. The imperial infantry, forming the sides of the rectangle, marched in sections of four, the front and rear walls deployed in extended line. In the leading wall were the 90th Foot, the Cameronians, and 94th, in the rear the 13th Foot, Somerset L.I., and 58th, on the right the 80th South Staffordshires, on the left a residue of 94th and the 21st. In line with the walls, trundled field guns and Gatlings.

Within the square, together with the general's staff, ammunition carriages and native troops, jogged the 17th Lancers and Dragoon Guards. Viewed against the panoramic sweep of the veld, it was a window of surrealistic pageantry. A low sun, glancing on enclosing ranks of scarlet infantry, the pennons of Lancers in blue uniforms lapelled with white, the great standards inscribed in gold, glinted on bayonets, cannon-brass and blaring musical instruments. The band of the 21st was playing 'The British Grenadiers'. Periodically, an order would be screamed to wheel left or right, or the blare of trumpets would halt the formation. Another blare would renew its forward march towards the royal kraal. Years afterwards, Zulu veterans would tell their children of the 'devil's diagram', the geometry that sealed their destruction.

Half a mile from Ulundi, Chelmsford halted the square on the hill between Nodwengu kraal and Mpande's grave. The defending impi was closing, massing in a great semi-circle, its tips flanking the square, its centre barring the path ahead. Each Zulu regiment had mustered its able-bodied survivors, replacing losses as it could with loyal, but unbloodied, lads. They approached slowly, stamping and banging their shields with their assegais, while remaining out of rifle range. There were few men in the Zulu ranks who had not learned the results of redcoat volley-fire at first hand. Those who had been at Isandhlwana had seen their comrades dropped in hundreds by a half-dozen isolated companies of British troops. Here, there were thirty-three companies in the walls alone, drawn shoulder to shoulder, four deep. And the centre of the square was packed with reserves, among them squadrons of regular cavalry.

Chelmsford's only fear was that the enemy would not charge. If the warriors held back and used, albeit poorly, what they had of firearms, they must do damage in his tight-knit formation. Accordingly, he used Buller's outlying irregulars to provoke the black regiments, while sending a mounted party to burn Nodwengu. At the same time, he pumped shell at Ulundi. A journalist with the division, Archibald Forbes of the *Daily News*, had offered 100-1 that the Zulus would not attack with so much against them. Melton Prior, the *Illustrated London News* artist, was in the square. He hoped Forbes was wrong. He wanted some good action sketches. He got them.

The Zulus charged shortly after 9 am. Their home villages had been burned, their kin slaughtered, their kraals plundered by the invader – and now their barracks and the dwellings of Ulundi were being destroyed before their eyes. It was better to die, urged the indunas, then stand and watch the destruction. They came slowly at first, chanting and stamping through the long grass; then, as Buller and the irregulars withdrew into the square for cover, the advance became an onrush of leaping, gesticulating warriors, brandishing assegais and loosing muskets. Mere boys and old men, those who had never before sighted a British line and those whose wounds from Isandhlwana and Kambula were still raw, all that remained of all the king's regiments charged in that last expression of national liberty, to immolate themselves in the deadly fire.

The first two ranks of the red wall were kneeling to offer the rear ranks a clear field. A thousand rifles bristled from each face of the square, plus rockets, Gatlings and artillery. They opened a barrage which rendered the battle a grim farce. Pathetically covered by hide shields, the warriors fell in their hundreds to bullet and case-shot.

> The Zulus [an intelligence report noted sparingly] pressed forward in their usual loose order, and sought to close with the British troops; but the steady and well-sustained fire of the infantry, supported by Gatlings and artillery, made this impossible, and at no point did they succeed in approaching nearer than thirty yards.

The closest attack was pressed against the right rear angle of the square, where two 9-pounders were flanked by Scots Fusiliers. It was smashed by oblique volley fire and point-blank cannonry, and the remnants of the charge fell back on Nodwengu.

Inside the square, where Lancers and Dragoons stood obediently at the heads of their horses, the less restrained irregulars raised themselves in their saddles to obtain a good view. Prior was working on his sketch pad. Buller was smoking a cigarette. Chelmsford and his staff watched the wavering Zulu regiments with satisfaction. Their cause had been lost from the start. Now, after twenty minutes of brutal devastation, they had had enough. As the artillery punished their retreat, Chelmsford unleashed his Lancers. Scores of warriors, caught before they could scramble to safety in the hills, were spitted by the galloping cavalry.

By the time the advance guard rode forward to Ulundi, at least a thousand Zulus were dead on the battleground. Ten of the Chelmsford's men had been killed. Such, as the historians of Empire would have it, was the 'glory' of Ulundi, the triumph of British arms. It was the conclusive stroke in the subjugation of the small Zulu nation. The royal kraal had been abandoned. The only inhabitants left in Ulundi were some women killed by the shell fire. There had been talk of a treasure hoard in the 'palace', but the only items discovered in Cetshwayo's mud residence were a pair of tusks, empty bottles, a pile of skins and, curiously, a large box full of London newspapers. Every dwelling in the community was now put to flame.

News of the definitive victory of the Zulu War was conveyed to the outside world by Forbes of the *Daily News*, who covered some 300 miles to Pietermaritzburg in a remarkable ride of fifty hours, his thigh swollen by a spent bullet, to get off his telegrams. One of them, reaching the 1st division on 7 June, put an end to Wolseley's hopes of striking the last blow. Chelmsford had achieved his aim. He had no intention of serving as Wolseley's subordinate, and no desire to see more of South Africa. The letter resigning his command was composed at Ulundi.

On 17 July, Wolseley addressed a gathering of chiefs in the subjugated kingdom with an assurance that they would enjoy themselves and 'become rich' under British supervision.

> Tell them [he ordered his interpreter], I am glad to see them because their coming here shows that they wish for peace, as the great queen does in whose name I speak. We have been at war with Cetshwayo, not with his people. We have beaten the king and burned his kraal. He is a fugitive in the bush, and shall never again rule in this land.

The chiefs raised their eyebrows. They *had* been at peace – until the British attacked them. War with Cetshwayo *was* war with his people. They had gone into battle shouting their loyalty. As a political expert, Wolseley was a good soldier.

If proof were needed of Zulu loyalty to Cetshwayo, it was amply demonstrated in the searches for the missing king, who, with a small party of his wives and children, eluded capture until the end of August. British search parties, torturing, threatening and bribing those they believed to possess information, could not induce a single Zulu to betray the whereabouts of the fugitives. Men were flogged, blindfolded and threatened with shooting Kraals were burned and cattle taken wholesale. Their owners would rather be murdered or ruined than talk. 'We tried everything,' wrote one officer. 'I had been a long time in Zululand, I knew the people and their habits, and although I believed they would be true to their king, I never expected such devotion.'

In the end, Cetshwayo was tracked to a small kraal in the Ngome forest. Sore and weakened from weeks of constant travelling, he invited the soldiers who surrounded his hut to enter and kill him. Instead, he was taken alive and exiled to Capetown. It was no more than an anti-climax, a postscript to the death of the kingdom founded by Shaka. Its symbolic end had already been performed by the doyenne of Zulu royalty, a dour centenarian named Mkabi. The first wife of Shaka's father, Senzangakona, Mkabi had witnessed the rise of the Zulu nation and survived to see it fall. On receiving news of the burning of Ulundi, she called her people together and faced them for the last time.

She had, she said, seen the glory of the Zulus. Now it had ended in disaster, and there was nothing for which to live. Whereupon the old lady raised a blade and, as her kindred watched, silently cut her own throat.

Wolseley ensured the disintegration of the Zulu realm by dividing it into thirteen artificial tribal units which he assigned arbitrarily to chiefs he considered reliable, among them men quite repugnant to many Zulus. Known in Natal as 'Wolseley's Kilkenny Cats', these included the trader Dunn, who had already proved himself traitor to the exiled king, and a Basuto named Hlubi whose people had fought for the British and were hated in Zululand. With a British resident who lacked the power to control the squabbling which ensued, the situation quickly veered towards anarchy.

In Britain, the considerable body of liberal opinion which had always opposed the Zulu War gained weight as the facts and circumstances became widely known, and the Government was strongly pressed to reinstate Cetshwayo, then living in what the *Morning Post* described as 'bare and unfurnished desolation' on the Cape. This, Chelmsford hastened to assure the press, would be a 'blunder of the gravest description ... The return of Cetshwayo to Zululand would at once restore the unity of the nation.'

The Government compromised. In January 1883, the king was returned to Ulundi, but his territorial restoration was only a half reality. Elsewhere, a chief named Sibebu, notorious for his hostility to the royal family, was installed as a counterpoise. Sibebu's conduct in Cetshwayo's absence – he had plundered not only the royal herds, but also the royal harem – had shocked even his own tribe. The confusion was compounded; civil war was inevitable.

Though widely loathed among the Zulus, Sibebu possessed a ruthlessness and military capacity foreign to the reinstated king. Further, while Cetshwayo was hamstrung by British officialdom, which denied him any effective force, Sibebu was encouraged to improve and expand his arms. For two months, the king's followers watched Sibebu gaining strength, then decided to act without the monarch's permission. On 30 March, warriors of the loyal Usutu group challenged Sibebu in battle, but were crushed by his superior generalship. Four months later, assisted by white hunters and adventurers, Sibebu pounced on Ulundi. Totally surprised, the king's men were annihilated and Cetshwayo, wounded, forced to seek safety with the British at Eshowe, where the resident commissioner treated him more or less as a prisoner.

Here, on 8 February 1884, Cetshwayo died. According to the account handed down by one of his wives, who was present:

> The king's dinner was brought to him by his servants, chiefly meat prepared by those hostile to him, for his own people had been forbidden by Osborn [the commissioner] to supply his food. Cetshwayo took a mouthful of meat ... this was followed by a terrible convulsion, his head dropped to one side and he sank back in a state of collapse; water was dashed over him and everything done to revive him, but he was dead.

The official verdict was that Cetshwayo died of a heart attack; most Zulus believe he was poisoned by Sibebu. Interestingly enough, the *Medical Times* published a letter shortly afterwards from a doctor who had examined the king during his period of exile.

> As ex-King Cetshwayo is stated to have died suddenly of fatty degeneration of the heart [it read], it may interest your readers

to know what was the state of his heart in August 1882 (eighteen months earlier). In ausculation the heart sounds were absolutely normal and the appended sphymographic tracing will show the healthy state of the arterial system.

At all events, Cetshwayo had had no chance of reviving his kingdom, a mere shadow of which devolved upon his heir, Dinizulu.

Dinizulu bribed the Boers into helping him to defeat Sibebu, but he could overcome neither the degeneration of the state nor the British. In 1887, Zululand was annexed to the Crown by the British Government. Implicated in two subsequent rebellions, Dinizulu stood no chance of restoring independence. The risings were quickly suppressed, but they had heightened government fears of an explosion of black discontent in South Africa, and a special commission was appointed in Natal to inquire into native administration.

Natal had played an important part on the British side during the Boer War, her politicians subsequently being prominent in the intercolonial negotiations preceding union. Meanwhile, native affairs had taken second place to party politics. War and agricultural set-backs had raised the cost of living, even for the Zulus, while a poll tax of £1 a head on all adult males, regardless of race, was a disproportionate burden on black Africans. The commission, recognising the faults in native administration, was impelled to the memorable conclusion:

> Since we can neither assimilate nor destroy them, political forethought and commonsense alike call for a settlement of the question on a broad, enlightened permanent basis.

For most white Natalians, the best answers to native problems were indeed to be found on a broad front, if enlightenment was disputable. The Union of 1910, for which they voted overwhelmingly, found Dinizulu in prison. He died in exile three years later, his people still awaiting any deep concern from their masters.

In 1929, Dr A. T. Bryant produced his first sociological work on the Zulus.

So far as we know [he wrote indignantly], no public fund or South African government, be it of the Union or of Natal, has ever considered the systematic collection and preservation of Zulu history as worth the outlay of one brass farthing or the expenditure of one hour's labour – a grim reflection of the white man's consistent and deliberate neglect of Native interests.

The dominating interests of the Union of South Africa were white interests. European settlers creamed off the best land, established and controlled cities and industries, looking to the so-called native locations, or reserves, for their labour force. The shortage and inferiority of land in the reserves obliged an increasing number of Africans to seek industrial employment, nevertheless the Zulus clung stubbornly to their tribal system and national life-style. In 1939, a report of the Native Farm Labour Committee recognised, as had Theophilus Shepstone sixty-five years earlier, that Zulu society was less than ideally organised to supply the labour upon which depended the industrial development of the Union.

In the period immediately following World War II, the native population of Natal (75 per cent of the total population) could be divided into two numerically equal groups: half lived on white men's farms, crown lands or the poor fringes of towns and cities; half still lived under tribal conditions on reserves. Though the Zulus fell mainly in the second category, their social structure and culture was beset by overcrowding and the inevitable pressures upon young men to migrate between the reserves and industrial occupation.

To the broader discontents of industrial revolution was added the fact that the Africans, while not entirely unrepresented, wholly lacked the political influence normal to a majority in democratic government, and, indeed, implicit in the traditional African systems, where unpopular rule was usually short-lived.

This situation, increasingly disturbing to intelligent Zulus, and particularly distasteful to the intellectual minority, was exacerbated by the swing to Apartheid. Since the creation of the Union, the constitutional status of the colonies had been eroded by central government. The struggle for power between whites now projected the old racial philosophy of the Boers in the so-called Nationalist party, a more liberal opposition asserting the constitutional position first defined by the British Government. In 1953, the Nationalists gained a Union majority. A year later, a revival of provincial liberalism was crushed in the Natal elections.

From now on, the policies of racial division and 'separate development' were unchecked. In April 1972, Zululand followed the Transkei to become the second semi-independent bantustan, or black 'homeland', in South Africa. Central to the evolution of Apartheid, the tribal homelands, with their vision of a distinctly limited autonomy, were greeted with scant joy by Africans who saw separate development as underdevelopment for the blacks.

On the eve of KwaZulu, as the new homeland was known, its first full-time prime minister, Chief Gatsha Buthelezi, displayed no illusions. 'I am a prime minister without a country and we are citizens of nowhere', he observed of a once cohesive black nation now fragmented into no less than twenty-nine pieces by white areas. There was no mistaking Zulu sentiments. One of the first institutions confirmed in KwaZulu was a national holiday to celebrate the memory of Shaka. Regimes are vulnerable; the spirit of a people is resilient.

BIBLIOGRAPHY

For those sufficiently interested by this brief text to explore the subject, and some allied topics, further, the following bibliography may suggest possibilities. No one seeking the history of the Zulu people can ignore Dr A. T. Bryant's great foundation work *Olden Times in Zululand and Natal*, which remains fascinating reading and a store of information. A more recent history of the Zulu and other Bantu people of South Africa is engrossingly related in Professor J. D. Omer-Cooper's scholarly *The Zulu Aftermath: A Nineteenth-Century Revolution in Bantu Africa*, an exciting example of the new African historiography which has emerged with the movement towards independence. An outstanding full-length narrative of the Zulu nation in the nineteenth century, and especially the Zulu War, is Donald R. Morris's *The Washing of the Spears – The Rise and Fall of the Zulu Nation*. Detailed in research, this fine piece of story-telling has the added interest of being diametrically opposed to my own interpretation of certain aspects of British conduct. Finally, as a postscript to the reign of Cetshwayo, C. T. Binns's *Dinizulu* provides an interesting account of the life of the ill-fated monarch's equally frustrated successor.

Ashe, Major, and Wyatt-Edgell, E. V. *The Story of the Zulu Campaign*. London, 1880.

Becker, Peter. *Rule of Fear – the Life and Times of Dingane*. London, 1964.

Binns, C. T. *The Last Zulu King – the Life and Death of Cetshwayo*. London, 1963.

Binns, C. T. *Dinizulu*. London, 1968.

Brookes, E. H., and Webb, C. de B. *A History of Natal*. Natal, 1965.

Bryant, A. T. *Olden Times in Zululand and Natal*. London, 1929.

Bryant, A. T. *The Zulu People*. Pietermaritzburg, 1949.

Colenso, Frances. *The Ruin of Zululand*. 2 vols. London, 1884.

Cory, George E. *The Rise of South Africa*. 5 vols. London, 1910-1919.

Dixie, Lady Florence. *A Defence of Zululand and its King*. London, 1882.

Elliot, W. J. *The Victoria Cross in Zululand and South Africa and How it Was Won*. London, 1882.

Escombe, H. *A Remonstrance on Behalf of the Zulu Chiefs*. Pietermaritzburg, 1908.

French, Gerald. *Lord Chelmsford and the Zulu War*. London, 1939.

Furneaux, Rupert. *The Zulu War: Isandhlwana and Rorke's Drift*. London, 1963.

Fynney, F. B. *The Zulu Army*. Pietermaritzburg, 1878.

Gibson, J. Y. *The Story of the Zulus*. Pietermaritzburg, 1903.

Gluckman, Max. *Analysis of a Social Situation in Modern Zululand*. Manchester, 1958.

Grant, James. *British Battles on Land and Sea*. 4 vols. London, 1899.

Haggard, H. Rider. *Cetshwayo and His White Neighbours*. London, 1882.

Hamilton Browne, G. *A Lost Legionary in South Africa*. London, 1912.

Hattersley, Alan F. *The British Settlement of Natal*. Cambridge, 1950.

Hattersley, Alan F. *Carbineer, The History of the Royal Natal Carbineers*. Aldershot, 1950.

Holt, H. P. *The Mounted Police in Natal*. London, 1913.

Hurst, G. T. *Short History of the Volunteer Regiments of Natal*. Durban, 1945.

Krige, Eileen. *The Social System of the Zulus*. Pietermaritzburg, 1957.

Lugg, H. C. *Historic Natal and Zululand*. Pietermaritzburg, 1949.

Bibliography

MacKinnon, J. P., and Shadbolt, S. *The South African Campaign, 1879*. London, 1880.

Mitford, Bertram. *Through the Zulu Country*. London, 1883.

Moodie, D. C. F. *Battles in South Africa Including the Zulu War*. Adelaide, 1879.

Morris, Donald R. *The Washing of the Spears – the Rise and Fall of the Zulu Nation*. London, 1965.

Mossop, G. *Running the Gauntlet*. London, 1932.

Norris-Newman, Charles. *In Zululand with the British Throughout the War of 1879*. London, 1880.

Omer-Cooper. J. D. *The Zulu Aftermath*. London, 1966.

Parr, H. H. *A Sketch of the Kafir and Zulu Wars*. London, 1880.

Ritter, E. A. *Shaka Zulu – the Rise of the Zulu Empire*. London, 1955.

Rogers, H. C. B. *Weapons of the British Soldier*. London, 1960.

Samuelson, R. C. A. *Long, Long Ago*. Durban, 1929.

Smith, E. W. *The Life and Times of Daniel Lindley (1801-1880)*. London, 1949.

Symons, Julian. *Buller's Campaign*. London, 1963.

Tisdal, E. E. P. *The Prince Imperial*. London, 1959.

Tomasson, W. H. *With the Irregulars in the Transvaal and Zululand*. London, 1881.

Walker, Eric A. *The Great Trek*. London, 1934.

Walker, Oliver. *Proud Zulu*. London, 1949.

Walker, Oliver. *Zulu Royal Feather*. London, 1961.

Wilmott, A. *A History of the Zulu War*. London, 1880.

Wood, Evelyn. *From Midshipman to Field Marshal*. London, 1906.

Wood, W. *Dingaan, King of the Zoolahs*. Cape Town, 1840.

Zululand, Précis of Information. (H.M.S.O.) London, 1886.

INDEX

Index

Gosset, Maj. Matthew, 65-6
Government *see* British Government
Graves, Maj. Shapland, 109

Hacket, Maj. Robert, 139
Harford, 59
Harness, Maj. Arthur, 49, 56, 61, 65-6, 104
Harrison, Qm. Gen. Richard, 149
Harward, Lieut. Henry, 122-3
Heliograph communication, 133-4
Helpmakaar, 99, 104
Hicks Beach, Sir Michael; Sec. of State for Colonies, 18-19, 105-7
Hitch, Pte. Frederick; V.C., 99, 103
Hlobane mountains, 115, 116, 124-31
Hook, Pte. Henry; V.C., 98, 102, 103
Hospital, Rorke's Drift, 89, 94, 97-9
19th Hussars, 109

InDlu-Yengwe regiment, 54, 69, 88, 94
Infantry, Imperial,
  Regular regiments,
    3rd, East Kent, 39, 45, 108, 133, 148
    4th, The King's Own, 39
    13th, Somersetshire Light, 39, 114, 139, 156
    21st, Royal Scots Fusiliers, 147, 148, 156
    24th, 39, 45, 48, 50, 56, 61, 62, 70, 74, 76, 79, 80, 82-3, 86, 88, 89, 97
    57th, West Middlesex, 106, 136, 142, 148
    58th, Rutlandshire, 147, 148, 156
    60th, King's Royal Rifle Corps, 136, 142, 148
    88th, Connaught Rangers, 148
    90th, Perthshire Volunteers, 39, 114, 138, 139, 156
    91st, Argyllshire Highlanders, 136, 142, 148
    94th, Connaught Rangers, 136, 147, 148
    99th, Duke of Edinburgh's Lanarkshire's, 108, 133, 148
Irregular regiments *see* European colonists and Kaffir levies
InGobamokhosi, 34, 67-8, 73, 75, 78-79, 81

InGlube tribe, 110
Intombe River, 120-3
Inyezane River, 109, 135, 136
IQwa tribe, 110
Isandhlwana,
  camp site, 55-8
  Chelmsford's absence,
    army strength, 70-1 73-4
    officers in charge, 61, 73
    Zulu attack, 74-83
  inquiry into disaster, 104-8
Isangqu regiment, 67, 78
Isipezi region, 60
Itelezi hill, 148-50
Ityotyosi River, 149

Jones, Pte. Robert; V.C., 99, 103
Jones, Pte. William; V.C., 99, 103

Kaffir levies, 70-1, 77, 88, 93, 109-111, 114, 124
  see also Browne, Dartnell, Durnford, and Lonsdale
Kambula camp, 116, 119, 124, 137-40
King's Royal Rifle Corps (60th foot regiment), 136, 142, 148
Kruger, Paul, 38, 57

Laager defence, 108, 121, 137, 139, 141
  neglected at Isandhlwana, 57, 74
17th Lancers regiment, 147, 148, 158
Le Tocq, Trooper, 150
Left column, 113-31
Levies *see* Kaffir levies
Lloyd, Llewellyn, 125-6
Lonsdale, Rupert de la Tour, 49, 50, 58-9, 62-3, 84-5
Louis Napoleon, Prince, 147, 148-52
Lowe, Col. Drury, 134
Luneberg district, 119-23
Lysons, Lieut. Henry; V.C., 126-31

McAllen, Sgt., 139
Magongo battle, 35
Mangeni camp, 63-5
Majias hill, 109
Malakatas range, 58
Manyanyoba, chief, 119-20, 121-3
Matyana, chief, 69
Mavumengwana, Gen., 54, 67

171

Index

Zululand

Ngome Forest

SWAZILAND

(KING
CAPTURED) *

Black Umfolosi River

Ulunc

Z U L

Pongola River

○ 2

1

To Derby ⟵

Luneberg

☆ Kambula

Itrotrosi River

Upoko River

Intombe River

5

4

3

Blood River

Balte Spruit

6

Utrecht

Buffalo River

Wakkerstroom

Dundee

TRANSVAAL

Newcastle

DRAKENBERG

Key to Heights   4. Munhla Hill   ☆ British Camps
  1. Zunguin   5. Inyayene Hill   ○ Battles
  2. Inhlobane   6. Doornberg   ⋯⋯ Approx. boundary
  3. Bembas Kop   7. Isepezi